Collins

Crossword Challenge Book 5

200 quick crossword puzzles

Published by Collins
An imprint of HarperCollins Publishers
Westerhill Road
Bishopbriggs
Glasgow G64 2QT

HarperCollins Publishers,
Macken House,
39/40 Mayor Street Upper,
Dublin 1,
D01 C9W8
Ireland

First Edition 2022

10 9 8 7 6 5 4 3 2

All puzzles supplied by Clarity Media Ltd

ISBN 978-0-00-846979-5

Printed in the UK using 100% Renewable Electricity at CPI Group (UK) Ltd

A catalogue record for this book is available from the British Library.

If you would like to comment on any aspect of this book, please contact us at the above address or online.
E-mail: puzzles@harpercollins.co.uk

This book is produced from independently certified FSC™ paper to ensure responsible forest management.

For more information visit: www.harpercollins.co.uk/green

CROSSWORD PUZZLES

PUZZLE 1

Across

1 Lessen (8)
5 Couple (4)
8 Beets (anag.) (5)
9 Large Israeli city (3,4)
10 Hawker (7)
12 Warm-blooded vertebrates (7)
14 Back up (7)
16 Decipher (7)
18 Abounding (7)
19 Effluent system (5)
20 Adds (4)
21 Great adulation (8)

Down

1 Liability (4)
2 Building exhibiting objects (6)
3 As might be expected (9)
4 Stomach crunches (3-3)
6 Heavy iron blocks (6)
7 Deeply respectful (8)
11 Process of scattering (9)
12 Official orders (8)
13 Howl (6)
14 Put on a play (6)
15 Deceive with ingenuity (6)
17 Wear away (4)

PUZZLE 2

Across

1 Thick mist (4)
3 Scrawl (8)
9 Mental strain (7)
10 Plant spike (5)
11 Total confusion (12)
13 Alcoholic drink (6)
15 Strangest (6)
17 Discreditable (12)
20 Abatement (5)
21 Pays no attention to (7)
22 Male comedian (8)
23 Trudge (4)

Down

1 Put into long-term storage (8)
2 Rejuvenate (5)
4 Bit of partly burnt wood (6)
5 Menacing (12)
6 Chocolate chewy cake (7)
7 Sea eagle (4)
8 List of books referred to (12)
12 Accented (8)
14 Reduce the volume (7)
16 Top aim (anag.) (6)
18 Precious stone (5)
19 Musical staff sign (4)

PUZZLE 3

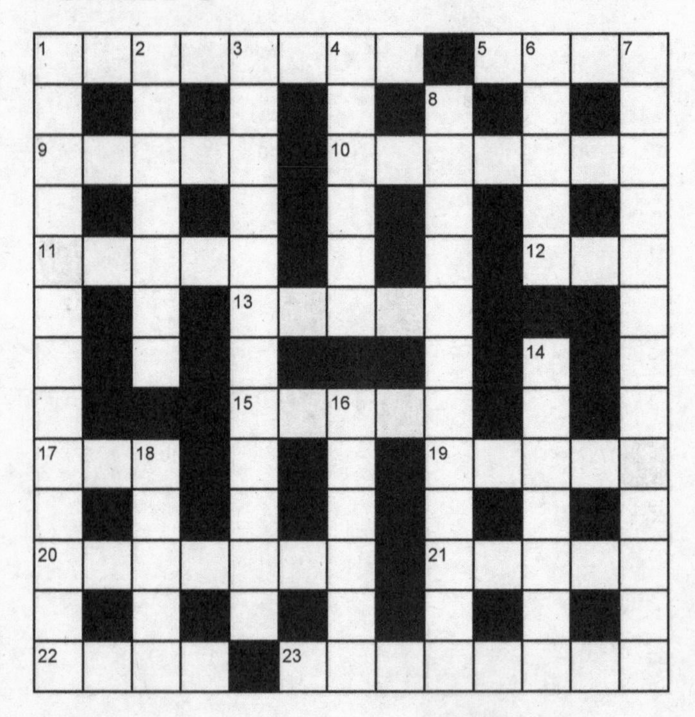

Across

1 Unjustly (8)
5 Hots (anag.) (4)
9 Self-evident truth (5)
10 Grapple with (7)
11 Dried kernel of the coconut (5)
12 Belonging to him (3)
13 Scheme intended to deceive (3-2)
15 Answer (5)
17 Popular beverage (3)
19 Set out (5)
20 Pamphlet (7)
21 Major African river (5)
22 Therefore (Latin) (4)
23 Worker (8)

Down

1 Inexplicable (13)
2 Turned over (7)
3 Limitless (12)
4 Opposite of highest (6)
6 Tie; snag (5)
7 Hidden store of valuables (8,5)
8 Highly abstract (12)
14 Clearly (7)
16 For the time being (3,3)
18 With a forward motion (5)

PUZZLE 4

Across

1 Thoroughly tidy the house (6,5)
9 Invigorating medicine (5)
10 Not bright; darken (3)
11 Find an answer to (5)
12 Not a winner (5)
13 Think deeply for a period of time (8)
16 Lacking confidence (8)
18 Narrow passageway (5)
21 Legend (5)
22 Feline (3)
23 Ethical (5)
24 Act of freeing from blame (11)

Down

2 Introductory piece of music (7)
3 Aims or purposes (7)
4 Large seabird (6)
5 In the area (5)
6 Mountain range in South America (5)
7 Likeness (11)
8 A change for the better (11)
14 Pamphlet (7)
15 Back pain (7)
17 Closer (6)
19 Milky fluid found in some plants (5)
20 Country in the Middle East (5)

PUZZLE 5

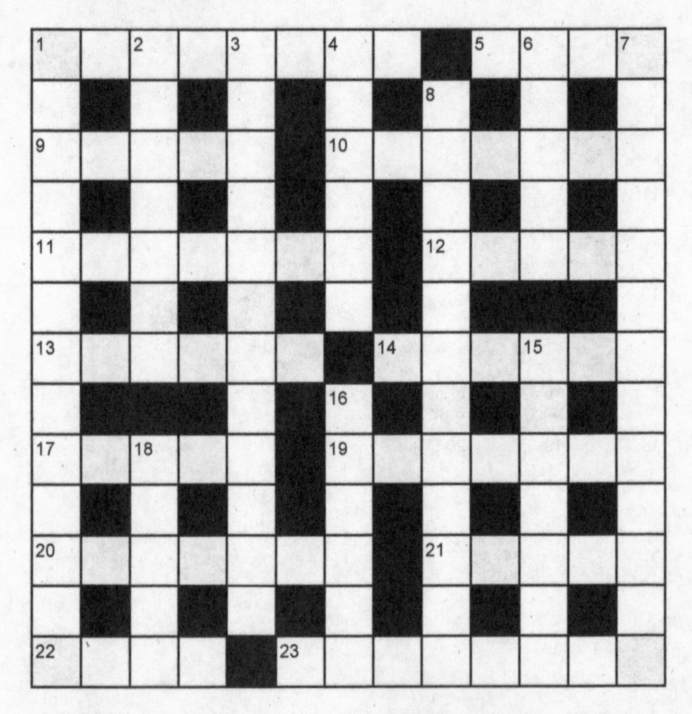

Across

1 Large terrier (8)
5 Chances of winning (4)
9 Sum; add up (5)
10 Exceptionally good (7)
11 Animal fat (7)
12 Brazilian dance (5)
13 Throes (anag.) (6)
14 Long mountain chain (6)
17 Machine; automaton (5)
19 Crush underfoot (7)
20 Devise beforehand (7)
21 Accustom (5)
22 Wooden crosspiece attached to animals (4)
23 Makes defamatory remarks (8)

Down

1 Account of one's own life (13)
2 Enhance a photo (7)
3 Intentionally (12)
4 Opposite of winners (6)
6 Belief in a god or gods (5)
7 Conscious knowledge of oneself (4-9)
8 Sweat (12)
15 Feeling of great joy (7)
16 Not written in any key (of music) (6)
18 Desolate (5)

PUZZLE 6

Across

1 Move about aimlessly (4)
3 Accommodating (8)
9 Obviously (7)
10 Very foolish (5)
11 Device for putting out fires (12)
14 Pull a vehicle (3)
16 First Pope (5)
17 Polite address for a man (3)
18 Unnecessarily careful (12)
21 Wading bird (5)
22 Floating wreckage (7)
23 Delaying (8)
24 Amaze (4)

Down

1 Reproduce (8)
2 Very skilled at something (5)
4 Purchase (3)
5 Imprudence (12)
6 Have a positive impact (7)
7 Men (4)
8 Clearness (12)
12 Extreme (5)
13 Male journalists (8)
15 Ditherer (7)
19 Start of (5)
20 Stimulate the appetite (4)
22 Enjoyable (3)

PUZZLE 7

Across

1 Most jolly (8)
5 Insect larva (4)
9 Walked up and down (5)
10 Plant of the parsley family (7)
11 Resolutely (12)
14 Smack (3)
15 Loop with a running knot (5)
16 Sticky substance (3)
17 Give a false account of (12)
20 Ask for; try to obtain (7)
22 Strange and mysterious (5)
23 Unpleasant smell (4)
24 Fighter in close combat (8)

Down

1 Amps (anag.) (4)
2 Narrate (7)
3 Freedom from control (12)
4 Pouch; enclosed space (3)
6 Direct competitor (5)
7 Extravagant fuss (8)
8 Altruism (12)
12 Search thoroughly for (5)
13 Sign of approval (6-2)
16 Not limited to one class (7)
18 Art gallery (5)
19 Beloved (4)
21 Bitumen (3)

PUZZLE 8

Across

1 Not at home (4)
3 Political meetings (8)
9 Platform (7)
10 Spacious (5)
11 Easy targets (7,5)
14 Not well (3)
16 Strong ringing sound (5)
17 High ball in tennis (3)
18 Very sad (12)
21 Evenly balanced (5)
22 Sets free or releases (7)
23 Quotidian (8)
24 Keeps on at (4)

Down

1 Type of word puzzle (8)
2 Valuable thing or person (5)
4 Limb (3)
5 Brusque and surly (12)
6 Breathing aid in water (7)
7 Utters (4)
8 In a creative manner (12)
12 Small particle (5)
13 Thinks about something continually (8)
15 Time off (7)
19 Capital of Ghana (5)
20 Give up one's rights (4)
22 North American nation (abbrev.) (3)

PUZZLE 9

Across

- **1** Remedy to a poison (8)
- **5** Volcano in Sicily (4)
- **9** Fishing net (5)
- **10** Foolish (7)
- **11** Policeman or woman (7)
- **12** Stage performer (5)
- **13** Provoke (6)
- **14** Long-legged rodent (6)
- **17** Accumulate (5)
- **19** A dancer or singer (7)
- **20** Writing fluid holder (7)
- **21** Health professional (5)
- **22** Negative votes (4)
- **23** Lack of hair (8)

Down

- **1** Tyrannical; domineering (13)
- **2** Movement of vehicles en masse (7)
- **3** Food shop (12)
- **4** Showy and cheap (6)
- **6** Act of stealing (5)
- **7** Aggressive self-assurance (13)
- **8** Uncurled (12)
- **15** Sudden increase (7)
- **16** Plant of the daisy family (6)
- **18** Foot joint (5)

PUZZLE 10

Across

1 Expel; drive out (4)
3 Pear-shaped fruits native to Mexico (8)
9 A general proposition (7)
10 Surprise result (5)
11 Destruction (12)
14 Mythical monster (3)
16 Gloomy (5)
17 Measure of length (3)
18 Triumphantly (12)
21 Cloak (5)
22 Shoulder blade (7)
23 Large stone (8)
24 Bill (4)

Down

1 Conventional (8)
2 Iron alloy (5)
4 Vitality (3)
5 Female fellow national (12)
6 Get rid of (7)
7 Locate or place (4)
8 Relating to numeric calculations (12)
12 Less common (5)
13 Listen to again (4,4)
15 Sophisticated hair style (7)
19 Foam or froth (5)
20 Moat (anag.) (4)
22 Used a chair (3)

PUZZLE 11

Across

1 Bedrooms (8)
5 Adhesive (4)
9 e.g. used a towel (5)
10 Routine dental examination (5-2)
11 Ruinously (12)
13 Sense of musical time (6)
14 Towards the rear of a ship (6)
17 Absurd (12)
20 Lenient (7)
21 Levy (5)
22 Stringed instrument (4)
23 Predator (anag.) (8)

Down

1 Auction offers (4)
2 Usefulness (7)
3 Antique; not modern (3-9)
4 Repeat from memory (6)
6 Bodies of water (5)
7 Evacuating (8)
8 One who takes part in a protest (12)
12 Hot and humid (8)
15 Imaginary line around the earth (7)
16 Sculptured figure (6)
18 Apply pressure (5)
19 Less than average tide (4)

PUZZLE 12

1		2		■	3	4		5		6		7
	■		■	8	■		■		■		■	
9							■	10				
	■		■		■		■		■		■	
11												■
	■	■	■		■		■		■		■	12
13		14				■	15					
	■		■		■	16	■		■	■	■	
■	17									18		
19	■		■		■		■		■		■	
20					■	21						
	■		■		■		■		■		■	
22								■	23			

Across

1 Facial disguise (4)
3 French bread stick (8)
9 Reasons for thinking something (7)
10 Leaves (5)
11 Mapmaker (12)
13 Painter (6)
15 Assent or agree to (6)
17 As a result (12)
20 Shrub fence (5)
21 Forbidden by law (7)
22 Quality of being holy (8)
23 Spheres (4)

Down

1 Sorcerer (8)
2 Track of an animal (5)
4 Soak up (6)
5 By chance (12)
6 Ancient warship (7)
7 Not difficult (4)
8 Not staying the same throughout (12)
12 Uses again (8)
14 Walked upon (7)
16 Screw up one's eyes (6)
18 Big cat (5)
19 Therefore (4)

PUZZLE 13

Across

1 Huge three-horned dinosaur (11)
9 Kind of beet (5)
10 Mock (3)
11 Relating to birth (5)
12 Loutish person (5)
13 Hitting hard (8)
16 Switch on (8)
18 Finely cut straw (5)
21 Grew fainter (5)
22 Not on (3)
23 Obsession (5)
24 Extend by inference (11)

Down

2 Tranquil (7)
3 One-eyed giant (7)
4 Explanation (6)
5 This date (5)
6 Soft fruit (5)
7 Snake (11)
8 Endorsed (11)
14 Trap for the unwary (7)
15 Protective helmet (4,3)
17 Doze (6)
19 Attach (5)
20 Thigh bone (5)

PUZZLE 14

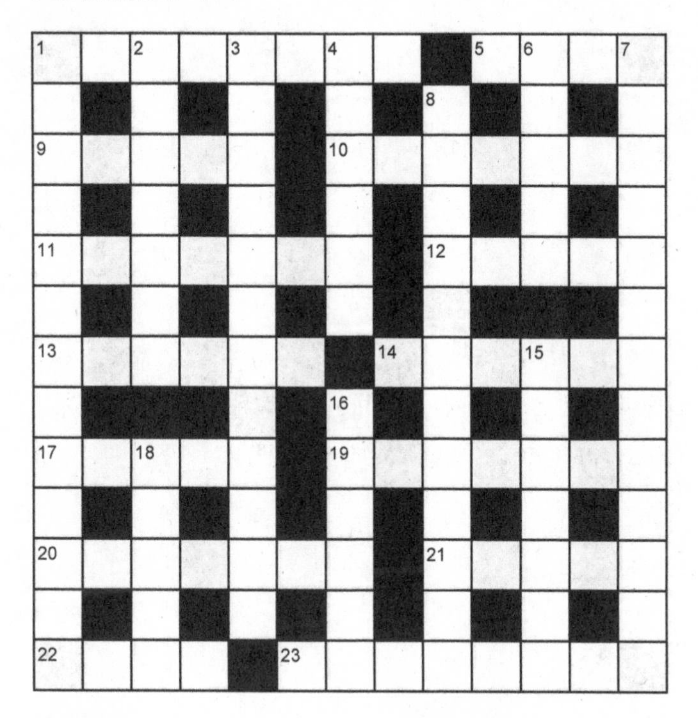

Across

1 Example (8)
5 Primates (4)
9 Movable helmet part (5)
10 Pear-shaped fruit native to Mexico (7)
11 Breastbone (7)
12 Cook meat in the oven (5)
13 Arch of the foot (6)
14 Positively charged atomic particle (6)
17 Saying (5)
19 Recites as a chant (7)
20 Stupid (7)
21 Shadow (5)
22 Near (4)
23 Frailty (8)

Down

1 Act of research (13)
2 Complex wholes (7)
3 Agreements; plans (12)
4 Asserts to be the case (6)
6 Public square (5)
7 Meteors (8,5)
8 Terrified or extremely shocked (6-6)
15 Plausible; defensible (7)
16 Mistake in snooker; blunder (6)
18 Chopping (5)

PUZZLE 15

Across

1 Alert and thinking cogently (5-6)
9 Climbing plant (3)
10 Rock group (5)
11 Grasp tightly (5)
12 Rustic (5)
13 Adolescent (8)
16 Extreme reproach (8)
18 Style of Greek architecture (5)
20 Show-off (5)
21 Coldly (5)
22 By way of (3)
23 Ending that leaves one in suspense (11)

Down

2 Stratum (5)
3 Coral reef (5)
4 Jostle (6)
5 Leave quickly and in secret (7)
6 Increase in size (7)
7 Magnifying instruments (11)
8 Occurring on the surface (11)
14 Uncommon (7)
15 Question after a mission (7)
17 Suffer destruction (6)
18 Most respected person in a field (5)
19 Variety show (5)

PUZZLE 16

Across

- **1** Makes a surprise attack on (8)
- **5** Matures (4)
- **9** Ape (abbrev.) (5)
- **10** River in South America (7)
- **11** Deduce or conclude (5)
- **12** Become firm (3)
- **13** In the middle of (5)
- **15** Royal (5)
- **17** Exclamation of contempt (3)
- **19** The Hunter (constellation) (5)
- **20** Flower-shaped competition award (7)
- **21** Intuitive feeling (5)
- **22** Puts down (4)
- **23** Surpass (8)

Down

- **1** Pertaining to building design (13)
- **2** Momentarily (7)
- **3** Large grocery stores (12)
- **4** Wore away gradually (6)
- **6** Merchandise; possessions (5)
- **7** Fairness in following the rules (13)
- **8** Garments worn in bed (12)
- **14** Narrower (7)
- **16** Rich cake (6)
- **18** Petulant (5)

PUZZLE 17

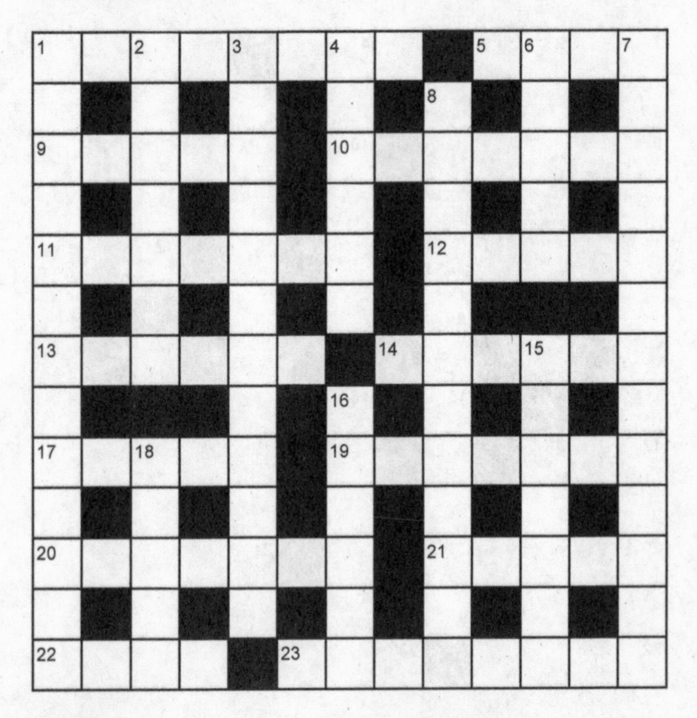

Across

1 Reassign (8)
5 Having inherent ability (4)
9 Electronic device (5)
10 Incidental result of a larger project (4-3)
11 Release someone from duty (7)
12 Lowest point (5)
13 Small whirlpools (6)
14 Rut (6)
17 Distinguishing character (5)
19 Severe (7)
20 Japanese warriors (7)
21 Understood with certainty (5)
22 Pull abruptly (4)
23 Person with an appreciation of beauty (8)

Down

1 Pitilessly (13)
2 Multiplied by two (7)
3 Ancestors (12)
4 Expelled from office (6)
6 Wide (5)
7 Fizz (13)
8 Evening dress for men (6,6)
15 Vanquished (7)
16 Value; respect (6)
18 Mortal (5)

PUZZLE 18

Across

1 Excited; lively (8)
5 Greek god of love (4)
9 Plantain lily (5)
10 One who places bets (7)
11 Very determined (6-6)
14 Signal for action (3)
15 Perhaps (5)
16 Joke (3)
17 Person's physical state (12)
20 Absorb all the attention of (7)
22 Bits of meat of low value (5)
23 Speck (4)
24 Very small unit of length (8)

Down

1 Having pains (4)
2 Create a positive feeling in a person (7)
3 Process of combining (12)
4 What a hen lays (3)
6 Governed (5)
7 Harsh; grating (8)
8 Able to use both hands well (12)
12 Country in North East Africa (5)
13 Frozen dessert (3,5)
16 Present for acceptance (7)
18 Period of darkness (5)
19 Chemical salt used in dyeing (4)
21 Our star (3)

PUZZLE 19

Across

1 Daydreamer (8)
5 Revolve around quickly (4)
9 Entertain (5)
10 Fatty substance (7)
11 Loving (12)
13 Fictional (4,2)
14 Talks (6)
17 Completely unaware of (12)
20 Momentum (7)
21 Fighter (5)
22 Ivy League university (4)
23 Opposites (8)

Down

1 Long periods of history (4)
2 Pleased (7)
3 Precondition (12)
4 Breaks apart forcibly (6)
6 Lively Bohemian dance (5)
7 Gibberish (8)
8 Unfriendly (12)
12 Exemption (8)
15 Incorporates into (7)
16 Individual (6)
18 Flower part; pales (anag.) (5)
19 Ancient boats (4)

PUZZLE 20

Across

1 Squeezes (8)
5 Drink greedily (4)
9 Acknowledged; assumed (5)
10 Open air controlled blaze (7)
11 Ordinary dress (5,7)
14 Mischievous sprite (3)
15 Brace (5)
16 Male person (3)
17 Break up into pieces (12)
20 Satisfy a desire (7)
22 Religious book (5)
23 Take a breath owing to astonishment (4)
24 Mean sect (anag.) (8)

Down

1 Gear wheels (4)
2 Surround entirely (7)
3 In a persuasive manner (12)
4 Recede (3)
6 Measure heaviness (5)
7 Estimating (8)
8 Without equal (12)
12 Stop (5)
13 Small sticks for starting a fire (8)
16 Liable to change (7)
18 Teams (5)
19 Animal skin (4)
21 Large period of time (3)

PUZZLE 21

Across

1 Clear (8)
5 Sullen (4)
9 Strength (5)
10 Enunciating (7)
11 A sense (5)
12 Inform upon (3)
13 Spear (5)
15 Rise to one's feet (3,2)
17 Small viper (3)
19 Sour substances (5)
20 Brings about (7)
21 Subject of a talk (5)
22 Invalid; void (4)
23 Debris (8)

Down

1 Process of taming an animal (13)
2 Imply (7)
3 Ability to acquire and apply knowledge (12)
4 Grotto (6)
6 Willow twig (5)
7 Virtuousness (13)
8 Sound of quick light steps (6-6)
14 Urgent (7)
16 Fine cloth (6)
18 Foot-operated lever (5)

PUZZLE 22

Across

1 Collide with (4)
3 Truly (8)
9 Get too big for something (7)
10 Outstanding (of a debt) (5)
11 Consumed (5)
12 Greek white wine (7)
13 Artefacts (6)
15 Prevented from moving (6)
17 Active during the day (7)
18 Welsh breed of dog (5)
20 Musical note (5)
21 Victory (7)
22 Qualified for by right (8)
23 Solely (4)

Down

1 Capable of being decomposed (13)
2 Short choral composition (5)
4 Ahead (6)
5 Malfunction or fail (of an electrical device) (5-7)
6 Point of view (7)
7 Autocratic (4-3-6)
8 Exceptional (12)
14 Noisiest (7)
16 Dress (6)
19 Manor (anag.) (5)

PUZZLE 23

Across

1 Look similar to (8)
5 Stated (4)
9 Type of plastic; record (5)
10 Remove clothes (7)
11 Tearing (7)
12 Greek writer of fables (5)
13 Catch or snare (6)
14 Firmly fixed (6)
17 Passageway (5)
19 Frequent customer (7)
20 Lines of equal pressure on maps (7)
21 Many times (5)
22 Pleasant (4)
23 Interpret in a certain way (8)

Down

1 Resonance (13)
2 Type of quarry (7)
3 Agreed upon by several parties (12)
4 Living room (6)
6 Asserts; affirms (5)
7 Act of vanishing (13)
8 Beneficial (12)
15 Support (7)
16 Wall painting; mural (6)
18 Indifferent to emotions (5)

PUZZLE 24

Across

1 Part of a sleeve (4)
3 Central American monkey (8)
9 Tidies (7)
10 Unit of heat (5)
11 Fault; mistake (5)
12 French dance (7)
13 Turbulence (6)
15 Sporting venues (6)
17 Biting sharply (7)
18 Expect; think that (5)
20 Cake decoration (5)
21 Inflexible and unyielding (7)
22 A period of 366 days (4,4)
23 Girl's toy (4)

Down

1 Following as a result (13)
2 Talent; ability (5)
4 Allocate a duty (6)
5 Inspiring action (12)
6 Perfumed (7)
7 Unpredictable (13)
8 Invigoratingly (12)
14 Copy (7)
16 Large lizard (6)
19 Adult insect (5)

PUZZLE 25

Across

4 Device that detects a physical property (6)
7 Wedge to keep an entrance open (8)
8 Chatter (3)
9 Large US feline (4)
10 Roofing material made of straw (6)
11 Attracts powerfully (7)
12 Lacking enthusiasm; weary (5)
15 Supplied by tube (5)
17 Gives way under pressure (7)
20 Reach (6)
21 Thin strip of wood (4)
22 Not (anag.) (3)
23 Supplemental part of a book (8)
24 A complex whole (6)

Down

1 Self-contained unit (6)
2 Animal (8)
3 Stammer (7)
4 Flatten on impact (5)
5 Exhaled audibly (6)
6 Stole from (6)
13 Having pH greater than 7 (8)
14 Root vegetables (7)
15 Flat dishes (6)
16 Silly tricks (6)
18 Impose or require (6)
19 Polite address for a woman (5)

PUZZLE 26

Across

- **1** Makes better (11)
- **9** Device that clears a car windscreen (5)
- **10** Sticky substance (3)
- **11** Hear a court case anew (5)
- **12** Guide a vehicle (5)
- **13** Something given to God (8)
- **16** Needed (8)
- **18** Ascends (5)
- **21** Prohibit (5)
- **22** Chemical element (3)
- **23** Capital of Japan (5)
- **24** Stood for (11)

Down

- **2** Powerful dog (7)
- **3** Legal practitioners (7)
- **4** Dispute the truth of (6)
- **5** Land measures (5)
- **6** Large bird of prey (5)
- **7** Confirm (11)
- **8** Needleworker (11)
- **14** Reduced in scope or length (3-4)
- **15** Commendation (7)
- **17** Calls forth (6)
- **19** Scorch (5)
- **20** Woodland spirit (5)

PUZZLE 27

Across

1 Composer or singer (8)
5 Heat up (4)
8 Give a solemn oath (5)
9 More straightforward (7)
10 Irreligious (7)
12 Pertaining to warfare (7)
14 Subdivision (7)
16 The gathering of crops (7)
18 Restaurant in a workplace (7)
19 Got up (5)
20 Right to hold property (4)
21 Expression of gratitude (5,3)

Down

1 Opposite of least (4)
2 Searcher (6)
3 Ink container put in a pen (9)
4 Attack (6)
6 In flower (6)
7 Someone skilled in shooting (8)
11 Ceramic material (9)
12 Fictitious (8)
13 European country (6)
14 Stink (6)
15 Stupidity (6)
17 Boyfriend (4)

PUZZLE 28

Across

1 One who lives through affliction (8)
5 Freezes over (4)
9 Lawful (5)
10 Fast musical composition (7)
11 Type of cloud (12)
13 Follows (6)
14 Arachnid (6)
17 Importance (12)
20 Stimulated; urged on (7)
21 Sorrowful (5)
22 Prophet (4)
23 Fetch (8)

Down

1 Marine flatfish (4)
2 Pulls back from (7)
3 Middleman (12)
4 Be preoccupied with something (6)
6 Gold measure (5)
7 Financial supporters (8)
8 Chair proctor (anag.) (12)
12 Continues obstinately (8)
15 State emphatically (7)
16 One under par in golf (6)
18 Loosely-woven cloth (5)
19 Computer memory unit (4)

PUZZLE 29

Across

1 Computer keyboard user (6)
7 Battered (8)
8 State of armed conflict (3)
9 Openly declared (6)
10 Comply with an order (4)
11 Appears (5)
13 Turn aside from a course (7)
15 Takes in (7)
17 Chuck (5)
21 Flightless bird (4)
22 Winged child (6)
23 Relieve or free from (3)
24 Large marsupial (8)
25 Capital of Russia (6)

Down

1 Absorbent cloths (6)
2 Buccaneer (6)
3 Melts (5)
4 Smears (7)
5 Knock down (8)
6 Do the same thing again (6)
12 Gin rooms (anag.) (8)
14 Vague and uncertain (7)
16 Relating to a wedding (6)
18 Heading on a document (6)
19 Glass opening in a wall (6)
20 Broom (5)

PUZZLE 30

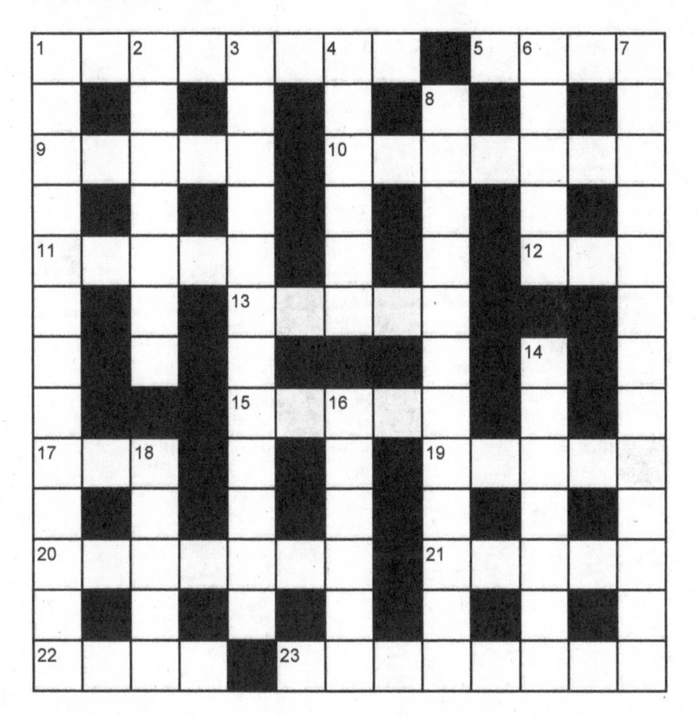

Across

1 Small pocket tool (8)
5 Moved through water (4)
9 Become ready to eat (of fruit) (5)
10 Period of prolonged dryness (7)
11 Bottle (5)
12 Male sheep (3)
13 Use to one's advantage (5)
15 Piece of code to automate a task (5)
17 e.g. pecan or cashew (3)
19 Roofed entrance to a house (5)
20 Faithfulness (7)
21 Snail (anag.) (5)
22 Word ending a prayer (4)
23 Competition participants (8)

Down

1 Miscellaneous equipment (13)
2 Pertaining to marriage (7)
3 Not catching fire easily (12)
4 Soft felt hat (6)
6 Gamble (5)
7 Process of transformation (of an insect) (13)
8 Metal device for removing tops (6,6)
14 Inhabitant of Mars (7)
16 Deep gorge (6)
18 Herb (5)

PUZZLE 31

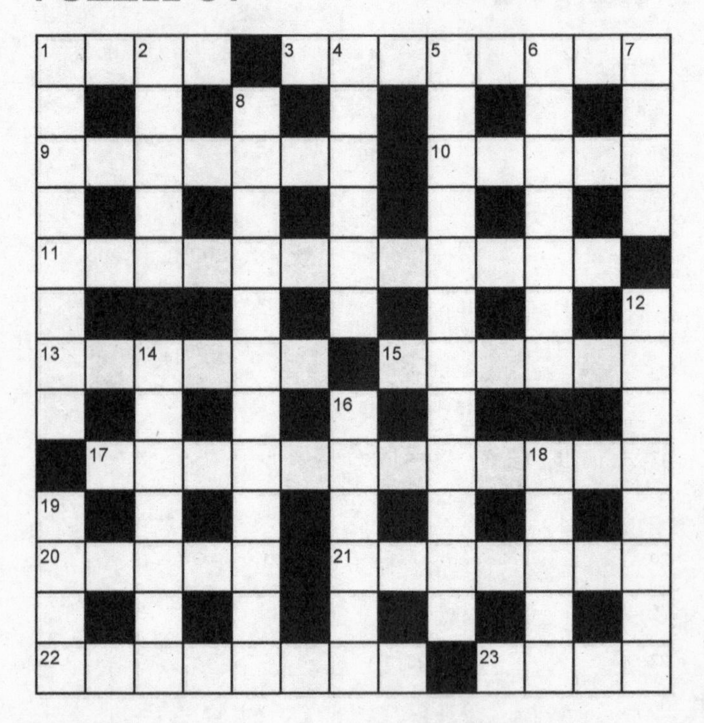

Across

1 Performs on stage (4)
3 White flakes in the hair (8)
9 Put in the ground (7)
10 Protective containers (5)
11 Easy to converse with (12)
13 Untamed; barbarous (6)
15 Propel with force (6)
17 Reallocate (12)
20 Ultimate (5)
21 Hit with the fist (7)
22 Curative medicines; sets right (8)
23 Sailing ship (4)

Down

1 Hand clapping (8)
2 Walk heavily and firmly (5)
4 Advance evidence for (6)
5 Formal announcements (12)
6 20th letter of the Greek alphabet (7)
7 Electrical safety device (4)
8 Determined (6-6)
12 Canine that herds animals (8)
14 Country in South East Asia (7)
16 Document fastener (6)
18 Wedding official (5)
19 From a distance (4)

PUZZLE 32

Across

1 Style and movement in art (6)
7 Radioactive element (8)
8 Month of the year (3)
9 Frozen water spear (6)
10 Vista (4)
11 Dank (5)
13 Assign (7)
15 A sudden impulse or desire (7)
17 Suit (5)
21 Spiciness (4)
22 Loan shark (6)
23 Knot with a double loop (3)
24 Ruler who has absolute power (8)
25 Open type of footwear (6)

Down

1 Extraterrestrial objects (6)
2 Purchasing (6)
3 Military walk (5)
4 Non-believer in God (7)
5 Cosmos (8)
6 Majestic (6)
12 Whirling motion (8)
14 Get as one's own (7)
16 Street (6)
18 Disallow; prevent (6)
19 Gardening tool (6)
20 Injures (5)

PUZZLE 33

Across

1 Sued (anag.) (4)
3 African country (8)
9 Unit of sound in a language (7)
10 Settle for sleep (of birds) (5)
11 Turn inside out (5)
12 Move; agitate (7)
13 Book of the Bible (6)
15 Manic (6)
17 Look something over (7)
18 Piece of furniture (5)
20 Store of hoarded wealth (5)
21 Pasta pockets (7)
22 Separate and distinct (8)
23 Vale (4)

Down

1 Unparalleled (13)
2 Run away with a lover (5)
4 Up-to-date and fashionable (6)
5 Regardless of (12)
6 Manufactured item (7)
7 Destroying microorganisms (13)
8 The proprietor of an eating establishment (12)
14 Burdensome (7)
16 Red wine (6)
19 Ruined; rendered inoperable (5)

PUZZLE 34

Across

1 Meeting where instructions are given (8)
5 Child's bed (4)
8 Water container (5)
9 Restrict (7)
10 Domestic fowl (7)
12 Approve or support (7)
14 Embarrassed (7)
16 Collection of sheets of paper (7)
18 Solid inorganic substance (7)
19 Courageous (5)
20 Decapod crustacean (4)
21 Process of sticking to a surface (8)

Down

1 Young child (4)
2 Supplied or distributed (6)
3 End of a digit (9)
4 See (6)
6 Recreate (6)
7 Well-rounded (8)
11 Unable to do something (9)
12 Justified in terms of profitability (8)
13 Basic metrical unit in a poem (6)
14 Mixed up or confused (6)
15 US state of islands (6)
17 Fastened with stitches (4)

PUZZLE 35

Across

1 Well-known sentence (11)
9 Small wood (5)
10 Command to a horse (3)
11 Draw off liquid from (5)
12 Loose stones on a slope (5)
13 Making big demands on something (8)
16 Strive (8)
18 Work hard (5)
21 Quoted (5)
22 Herb; regret (3)
23 Area of sand (5)
24 Having celebrities in attendance (4-7)

Down

2 Yearbook (7)
3 Blood relative (7)
4 Quantum of electromagnetic radiation (6)
5 Staggers (5)
6 Sweetening substance (5)
7 Parakeets (11)
8 Calm and sensible (5-6)
14 Ate a midday meal (7)
15 Disturb (7)
17 Cruel ruler (6)
19 Representative (5)
20 Underground enlarged stem (5)

PUZZLE 36

Across

1 Curved shapes (4)
3 Pertaining to Spain (8)
9 Saying (7)
10 Certain to end in failure (2-3)
11 Made a mistake (5)
12 Surround with armed forces (7)
13 Reprimand (6)
15 Religious leader (6)
17 Flog; whip (7)
18 Extra component (3-2)
20 Cleanse the body (5)
21 Italian red wine (7)
22 Revealing a truth (8)
23 Cut of meat (4)

Down

1 Understandable (13)
2 Group of singers (5)
4 Drink (6)
5 State of the USA (12)
6 This starts on 1st January (3,4)
7 Attitude of superiority or arrogance (13)
8 Main premises of a company (12)
14 Highest vantage point of a building (7)
16 Visible warning device (6)
19 Wild dog of Australia (5)

PUZZLE 37

Across

1 Bring together (8)
5 Edible fruit with a distinctive shape (4)
9 Humming (5)
10 Disavowals; rebuttals (7)
11 Disregarding the rules (5,3,4)
14 Draw (3)
15 Snow leopard (5)
16 Type of statistical chart (3)
17 Revival of something (12)
20 Final parts of stories (7)
22 Flat-bottomed boat (5)
23 Require (4)
24 Pennant (8)

Down

1 Slightly open (4)
2 Sleep (4-3)
3 Female singing voice (5-7)
4 Was in first place (3)
6 Fill with high spirits (5)
7 Flower-shaped competition awards (8)
8 Not discernible (12)
12 Tight; taut (5)
13 Large fish (8)
16 Schedule of activities (7)
18 Move sideways (5)
19 Change direction suddenly (4)
21 Ease into a chair (3)

PUZZLE 38

Across

1 In the open air (8)
5 Piece of evidence (4)
9 Confusion (3-2)
10 Agitate (7)
11 Atomic particle (7)
12 Increase in size (5)
13 Israeli monetary unit (6)
14 Birthplace of St Francis (6)
17 Short bolt or pin (5)
19 Tragedy by Shakespeare (7)
20 Burdensome work (7)
21 Angry (5)
22 Prickly plant with fragrant flowers (4)
23 Conduct business (8)

Down

1 Person performing official duties (13)
2 Fitting (7)
3 Derived from past events (12)
4 Managing (6)
6 Parasitic insect (5)
7 Ornamentation (13)
8 Sample of a larger group (5,7)
15 Japanese flower arranging (7)
16 Marble (anag.) (6)
18 Small bottles (5)

PUZZLE 39

Across

1 Food containers (4)
3 Padding (8)
9 Nattier (anag.) (7)
10 Lover of Juliet (5)
11 Alcoholic drink made from apples (5)
12 Feeling of vexation (7)
13 Capital of Canada (6)
15 Season of the Church year (6)
17 Becoming submerged (7)
18 Lumberjack (5)
20 Became less intense (5)
21 Put in order (7)
22 Reference point; norm (8)
23 Jealousy (4)

Down

1 Awareness (13)
2 Observed (5)
4 From that place (6)
5 Pungent gas used as a preservative (12)
6 Steep in; engross (7)
7 Amiably (4-9)
8 Lacking tolerance or flexibility (6-6)
14 Country in North Africa (7)
16 Less attractive (6)
19 Pallid (5)

PUZZLE 40

Across

1 Frustrating (11)
9 Increase the running speed of an engine (3)
10 Criminal (5)
11 Destitute (5)
12 Endures (5)
13 Estrange (anag.) (8)
16 Extremely lovable (8)
18 Type of coffee drink (5)
20 Sycophant (5)
21 Underwater breathing device (5)
22 Every (3)
23 Type of artist (11)

Down

2 Donates (5)
3 Fissures (5)
4 Measure of loudness (6)
5 Tax imposed on ships (7)
6 Digit (7)
7 Wonderfully (11)
8 Obscurely (11)
14 Cigarette constituent (7)
15 Look after an infant (7)
17 Small pit or cavity (6)
18 Intended (5)
19 Group of students; category (5)

PUZZLE 41

Across

4 Wanders off; drifts (6)
7 Gigantic (8)
8 Taxi (3)
9 Overly submissive (4)
10 Enforce compliance with (6)
11 Buying and selling (7)
12 Small pier (5)
15 Jumps in the air (5)
17 Sad (7)
20 Without ethics (6)
21 Snake-like fish (pl.) (4)
22 Deep hole in the ground (3)
23 Shortage (8)
24 Pieces of crockery (6)

Down

1 Show-off (6)
2 Excessively emotional (6,2)
3 Allots (7)
4 Hits with the hand (5)
5 Upward slope (6)
6 Tunnel under a road for pedestrians (6)
13 Fade away (8)
14 Reveal (7)
15 Drank with the tongue (6)
16 Lessens (6)
18 Courteous (6)
19 Worthless material (5)

PUZZLE 42

Across

1 Moist (4)
3 Type of Eurasian carp (8)
9 Designer of trendy clothes (7)
10 Artificial waterway (5)
11 Mixture of gases we breathe (3)
12 Contest (5)
13 Shine brightly (5)
15 Makes (a sound) (5)
17 Compel (5)
18 Snip (3)
19 Type of coffee drink (5)
20 Evaded (7)
21 Christmas season (8)
22 Type of high-energy radiation (1-3)

Down

1 Repugnantly (13)
2 District council head (5)
4 Series of eight notes (6)
5 Withdraw from service (12)
6 Caused to burn (7)
7 Unenthusiastically (4-9)
8 Conflict of opinion (12)
14 Pertaining to matrimony (7)
16 Away from the coast (6)
18 Cared (anag.) (5)

PUZZLE 43

Across

1 Reliable (11)
9 Extreme fear (5)
10 Amp (anag.) (3)
11 Unconditional love (5)
12 Vertical part of a step (5)
13 Capable of being satisfied (8)
16 Highly seasoned smoked beef (8)
18 Private room on a ship (5)
21 Pulsate (5)
22 Religious sister (3)
23 Single-edged hunting knife (5)
24 Acting out a part (4,7)

Down

2 Meals (7)
3 Motorcycle attachment (7)
4 Wretched (6)
5 Detection technology (5)
6 Church songs (5)
7 Semi-transparent (11)
8 Considerable (11)
14 Majestic (7)
15 Sheikhdom in the Persian Gulf (7)
17 Open declaration of affirmation (6)
19 Stringed instrument (5)
20 Male aristocrat (5)

PUZZLE 44

Across

1 Discover (6)
7 Extension of a debt (8)
8 Mammal with a bushy tail (3)
9 Refrigerator compartment (6)
10 Steep and rugged rock (4)
11 Stiff with age (5)
13 Part of a chair (7)
15 People (7)
17 The prevailing fashion (5)
21 Haul (4)
22 Expression of praise (6)
23 Sorrowful (3)
24 Foul-smelling (8)
25 Hankers after (6)

Down

1 Disagree (6)
2 Poisonous substances (6)
3 Biter (anag.) (5)
4 Cure-alls (7)
5 Musical composition (8)
6 Decomposes (6)
12 Struggling (8)
14 Cherubic (7)
16 Fairness (6)
18 Hot spring (6)
19 Discharges (6)
20 Mournful poem (5)

PUZZLE 45

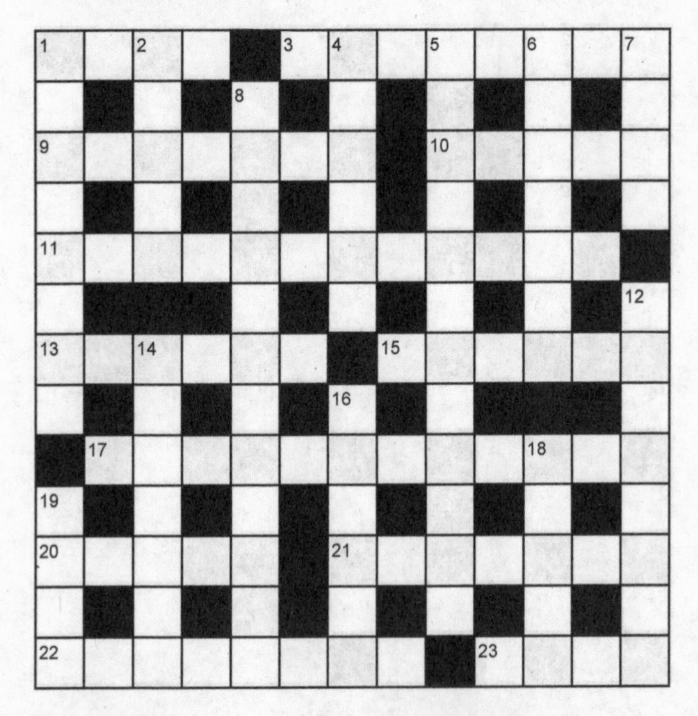

Across

1 Knuckle of pork (4)
3 Precise and clear (8)
9 Simple sugar (7)
10 Sheltered places (5)
11 Joyously unrestrained (4-8)
13 Military forces (6)
15 One who manages finances at a college (6)
17 Contradictory (12)
20 Elevators (5)
21 Formally approved (7)
22 Lessening (8)
23 Dairy product (4)

Down

1 Large cask (8)
2 Held on to something tightly (5)
4 Written in verse (6)
5 Extension (12)
6 e.g. daisies and roses (7)
7 Group of actors in a show (4)
8 In a carefree manner (12)
12 Amicable (8)
14 Attentive; conscious of (7)
16 Wrench an ankle (6)
18 Bungle (5)
19 Wingless jumping insect (4)

PUZZLE 46

Across

1 School break (8)
5 Glass ornament; small ball (4)
9 White waterbird (5)
10 Japanese massage technique (7)
11 Formation of troops (7)
12 Wild and untamed (5)
13 Contributes information (6)
14 Pertaining to vinegar (6)
17 Prevent (5)
19 Vent for molten lava (7)
20 Separated; remote (7)
21 Individual things (5)
22 Longest river (4)
23 Renounce (8)

Down

1 Intent (13)
2 Zeppelin (7)
3 Chatter (6-6)
4 Pondering (6)
6 Go in (5)
7 Betrayer (6-7)
8 Tricky elements; obstacles (12)
15 Circus apparatus (7)
16 Exaggerate (6)
18 Frame for holding an artist's work (5)

PUZZLE 47

Across

1 Persistent harassment (11)
9 Friendship (5)
10 Owed and payable (3)
11 Undergarments (5)
12 Trunk of the body (5)
13 Provided a service (8)
16 One liquid dispersed in another (8)
18 Teacher (5)
21 Repository (5)
22 Put a question to (3)
23 Smooth cream of vegetables (5)
24 One who held a job previously (11)

Down

2 Deleting (7)
3 Broke into pieces (7)
4 Trite remark (6)
5 Secret rendezvous (5)
6 More mature (5)
7 Respectful (11)
8 Divisor (11)
14 Flying vehicles without engines (7)
15 River of South East Africa (7)
17 A system of measurement (6)
19 Buyer (5)
20 Swift (5)

PUZZLE 48

1 2 3 4 5 6 7
8
9 10
11
12
13 14 15
16
17 18
19
20 21
22 23

Across

1 Circuitous (8)
5 Finish (4)
9 Leaf of parchment (5)
10 Throw into disorder (7)
11 Small garden carts (12)
13 Aircraft housing (6)
14 Line of equal pressure on a map (6)
17 Opposite of amateur (12)
20 Be subjected to (7)
21 Quavering sound (5)
22 Items that unlock doors (4)
23 Spacecraft (8)

Down

1 Doubtful (4)
2 Marine mammal (7)
3 Large Brazilian city (3,2,7)
4 Tiny bits of bread (6)
6 Ballroom dance (5)
7 Gratification (8)
8 Marksman (12)
12 Burrowing ground squirrel (8)
15 Expecting prices to fall (7)
16 Bodyguard (6)
18 Strangely (5)
19 Move wings; flutter (4)

PUZZLE 49

Across

1 Beyond acceptability (3,2,6)
9 Very informal phrases (5)
10 Born (3)
11 Climb onto (5)
12 Bundle of wheat (5)
13 Humility and gentleness (8)
16 Huge (8)
18 Dreadful (5)
21 Tool for boring holes (5)
22 Bed for a baby (3)
23 Of definite shape (5)
24 Amazing (11)

Down

2 Restless (7)
3 Driving out (7)
4 Talks excessively about one's talents (6)
5 Strong desires (5)
6 Closely compacted (5)
7 A recollection (11)
8 Confident (4-7)
14 Width (7)
15 Harden (7)
17 Central parts of cells (6)
19 Outdoor fundraising events (5)
20 Rope with a running noose (5)

PUZZLE 50

Across

1 Regretted (4)
3 Unexpectedly (8)
9 Type of photographic shot (5-2)
10 Heavily loaded (5)
11 Lack of practical knowledge (12)
14 Make a mistake (3)
16 Arm joint (5)
17 Cry (3)
18 Make a guess that is too high (12)
21 Cloth woven from flax (5)
22 Urges strongly (7)
23 People who provide massages (8)
24 Pointer on a clock (4)

Down

1 Accepted (8)
2 Call forth (5)
4 Bite sharply (3)
5 Boxing class division (12)
6 Lessens (7)
7 Trigonometric function (4)
8 Re-emergence (12)
12 Loose outer garments (5)
13 Completely preoccupied with (8)
15 Deep gorges (7)
19 Main artery (5)
20 Shut with force (4)
22 What one hears with (3)

PUZZLE 51

Across

1 Designed for usefulness (11)
9 Annoy (3)
10 Buffalo (5)
11 Escape from (5)
12 Fop (5)
13 Adjoining (8)
16 Beekeeper (8)
18 Exhibited (5)
20 Youngsters aged 13 - 19 (5)
21 Three-note chord (5)
22 Part of a curve (3)
23 Philosophical doctrine (11)

Down

2 Symbol (5)
3 Entrance hall (5)
4 Sampled (food) (6)
5 Regeneration (7)
6 Guarantees (7)
7 Of a generous disposition (4-7)
8 Branch of physics (11)
14 Absence of sound (7)
15 One who holds property for another (7)
17 Reactive metal (6)
18 Carrying chair (5)
19 Gemstones (5)

PUZZLE 52

Across

1 Money in notes or coins (4)
3 Assimilate again (8)
9 Not as quiet (7)
10 Word of farewell (5)
11 Excess (5)
12 Game played on a sloping board (7)
13 Flourish (6)
15 Dock for small yachts (6)
17 Capital of the US state of Georgia (7)
18 Monster with nine heads (5)
20 Balearic party island (5)
21 Agrees (7)
22 Disregards (8)
23 Item of footwear (4)

Down

1 Close mental application (13)
2 Avoid; garment (5)
4 Continent (6)
5 Forcible indoctrination (12)
6 Art of paper-folding (7)
7 Spicy fish stew (13)
8 Drawback (12)
14 Turning over and over (7)
16 Surgical knife (6)
19 Flour and water mixture (5)

PUZZLE 53

Across

1 Furry nocturnal mammals (8)
5 Put down gently (4)
9 Embed; type of filling (5)
10 Infective agents (7)
11 Cut up wood (7)
12 Benefactor (5)
13 Lower (6)
14 Firmly established (6)
17 Smell (5)
19 Assign (7)
20 Malady (7)
21 Speak in public without preparation (2-3)
22 Dons (anag.) (4)
23 Participant in a meeting (8)

Down

1 Rebirth in a new body (13)
2 Substance such as a gel or emulsion (7)
3 International multi-sport event (7,5)
4 US state whose capital is Carson City (6)
6 Crime of setting something on fire (5)
7 Disreputable (13)
8 Most prominent position (5,2,5)
15 Rotated quickly (7)
16 Breed of hound (6)
18 Lubricated (5)

PUZZLE 54

Across

1 Succulent (4)
3 Pepper plant (8)
9 Distribute illicitly (7)
10 Possessed (5)
11 Total destruction (12)
13 East (6)
15 Stop talking (4,2)
17 Type of contest (12)
20 Directly opposite in character (5)
21 Resistance to change (7)
22 Decreasing (8)
23 In a lazy way (4)

Down

1 Breed of retriever (8)
2 Item of cutlery (5)
4 Attendants upon God (6)
5 Cheated someone financially (5-7)
6 Make by mixing ingredients (7)
7 Method; fashion (4)
8 Using both letters and numerals (12)
12 Moment of great revelation (8)
14 Breathed in (7)
16 Outer part of a bird's wing (6)
18 Despised (5)
19 Box (4)

PUZZLE 55

Across

- **4** Come off the tracks (6)
- **7** Capable of happening (8)
- **8** Sticky yellowish substance (3)
- **9** Corner (4)
- **10** Type of rhododendron (6)
- **11** Lives in (7)
- **12** Annoying (5)
- **15** Ship frames (5)
- **17** Hot-tasting food dishes (7)
- **20** Atmospheric phenomenon (6)
- **21** Self-righteous person (4)
- **22** Relations (3)
- **23** Reads out (8)
- **24** Short trip to perform a task (6)

Down

- **1** Pasta strip (6)
- **2** Exceptional (8)
- **3** Wears away (7)
- **4** Decomposition (5)
- **5** Forever (6)
- **6** State of great comfort (6)
- **13** e.g. from Italy or Spain (8)
- **14** Large island of Indonesia (7)
- **15** Shout down; harass (6)
- **16** Lender (6)
- **18** US rapper (6)
- **19** Dog (5)

PUZZLE 56

Across

1 Japanese sport (4)
3 Shrill (8)
9 Forgive (7)
10 Friend (Spanish) (5)
11 Absolute authority in any sphere (12)
14 Enemy (3)
16 Prophets (5)
17 Deranged (3)
18 Graphical (12)
21 Nose of an animal (5)
22 Change the form of something (7)
23 Changing (8)
24 Document of ownership (4)

Down

1 Deadlock (5-3)
2 Agreeable sound or tune (5)
4 Frozen water (3)
5 Re-evaluation (12)
6 One of the platinum metals (7)
7 Increase in size (4)
8 Having keen vision (5-7)
12 Last Greek letter (5)
13 Taught (8)
15 One event in a sequence (7)
19 At that place; not here (5)
20 Continent (4)
22 Metal container (3)

PUZZLE 57

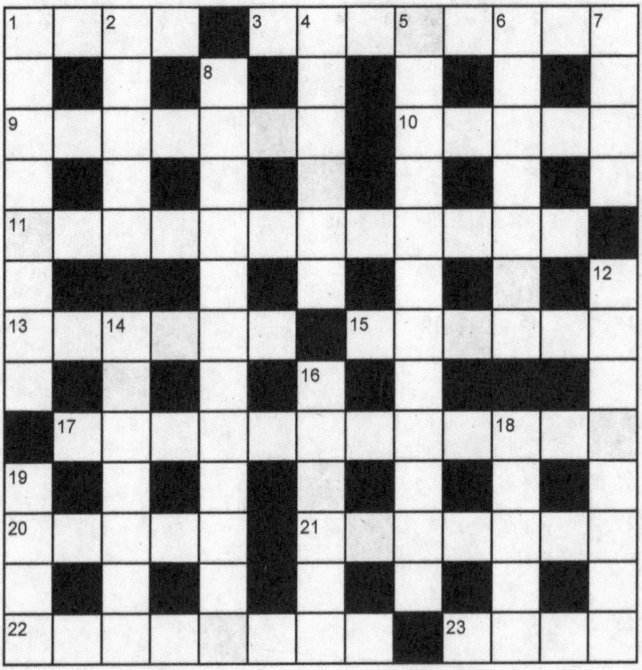

Across

1 Person who receives guests (4)
3 Boxing (8)
9 Far-reaching; thorough (7)
10 Appear suddenly (3,2)
11 Quarrelsome and uncooperative (12)
13 Event which prepares for another (6)
15 Large beam (6)
17 Occurring at the same time (12)
20 Spin quickly (5)
21 Irritating; hankering (7)
22 Social insect (8)
23 Allot a punishment (4)

Down

1 Printed version of data on a computer (4,4)
2 Country in North East Africa (5)
4 Different from (6)
5 Impudence (12)
6 Seize and take legal custody of (7)
7 Brood (4)
8 Now and then (12)
12 Preliminary speech (8)
14 e.g. hate or joy (7)
16 Limited (6)
18 Hackneyed (5)
19 State of the USA (4)

PUZZLE 58

Across

1 Rebuild (11)
9 Longest river in Europe (5)
10 Wily (3)
11 Skirmish (5)
12 Doctor (5)
13 Salad sauce (8)
16 Person highly skilled in music (8)
18 Popular sport (5)
21 Musical instrument (5)
22 Tree (3)
23 Worship; venerate (5)
24 Make in bulk (4-7)

Down

2 Changes gradually (7)
3 Side of a coin bearing the head (7)
4 Morose (6)
5 Furnish with new weapons (5)
6 Enclosed (5)
7 The military (5,6)
8 Occurring at the same time (11)
14 Regular salary (7)
15 Pertaining to plants (7)
17 Situated within a building (6)
19 Third Greek letter (5)
20 Resay (anag.) (5)

PUZZLE 59

Across

1 Hairdressing establishments (6)
7 Prodigal (8)
8 Athletic facility (3)
9 Picture produced from many small pieces (6)
10 Petty quarrel (4)
11 Cleans (5)
13 Lying (7)
15 Embryonic root (7)
17 Hidden storage space (5)
21 Audacity (4)
22 Son of one's brother or sister (6)
23 Container (3)
24 Pessimistic (8)
25 Woodcutter (6)

Down

1 Autographed something for a fan (6)
2 Assumed propositions (6)
3 Perspire (5)
4 Able to read minds (7)
5 Segment of the spinal column (8)
6 Seabird (6)
12 Multiplying by three (8)
14 Angled; biased (7)
16 River in South America (6)
18 Cattle herder (6)
19 Magical potion (6)
20 Notices (5)

PUZZLE 60

Across

- **1** Legal document (4)
- **3** Sears (8)
- **9** Hermit (7)
- **10** Floral leaf (5)
- **11** Collection of paper (3)
- **12** Lift up (5)
- **13** Relating to vision (5)
- **15** Cuts slightly (5)
- **17** Finished (5)
- **18** Insect which collects pollen (3)
- **19** Harsh and serious (5)
- **20** Floating; cheerful (7)
- **21** Held out against (8)
- **22** Tax (4)

Down

- **1** Computer program for writing documents (4,9)
- **2** Decal (anag.) (5)
- **4** Recognition (6)
- **5** Consequence of an event (12)
- **6** Smacking (7)
- **7** Obviously (4-9)
- **8** Environment (12)
- **14** Symptom of blushing (7)
- **16** Small round stone (6)
- **18** Fire (5)

PUZZLE 61

1		2		3		4		■	5	6		7
	■		■		■		■	8	■		■	
9					■	10						
	■		■		■		■		■		■	
■	11											
12	■		■		■		■		■	■	■	
13						■	14			15		
	■	■	■		■	16	■		■		■	
17		18										■
	■		■		■		■		■		■	19
20							■	21				
	■		■		■		■		■		■	
22				■	23							

Across

1 Written guarantee (8)
5 Main island of Indonesia (4)
9 Sailing vessel (5)
10 Endurance (7)
11 Insubordination (12)
13 Higher in rank (6)
14 Free from danger (6)
17 Action of breaking a law (12)
20 Do repeatedly (7)
21 Ring solemnly (5)
22 Deities (4)
23 Portable device to keep the rain off (8)

Down

1 Routes; methods (4)
2 Disturbance; commotion (7)
3 Relating to horoscopes (12)
4 Checked; examined (6)
6 Pertaining to bees (5)
7 Roused from sleep (8)
8 Skilled joiner (12)
12 Praising (anag.) (8)
15 Hide (7)
16 Shining (6)
18 Released from jail (5)
19 Earnest appeal (4)

PUZZLE 62

Across

1 Unattractive (4)
3 Getting away from (8)
9 Opposite (7)
10 Christmas song (5)
11 Did possess (3)
12 Rental agreement (5)
13 Customary practice (5)
15 e.g. spaghetti (5)
17 Game fish (5)
18 Gang (3)
19 Shout of appreciation (5)
20 Act of awakening from sleep (7)
21 Letting off (8)
22 Small island (4)

Down

1 Unsuitable for living in (13)
2 Cherished (5)
4 Afternoon snooze in Spain (6)
5 Rate of increase in speed (12)
6 Intrusions (7)
7 50th anniversary of a major event (6,7)
8 Excessively forward (12)
14 Mundane (7)
16 Stress; pull a muscle (6)
18 Thin fogs (5)

PUZZLE 63

Across

1 Irritable (3-8)
9 Tree of the genus Quercus (3)
10 Melodies (5)
11 Golf clubs (5)
12 Darken (5)
13 News journalist (8)
16 First in importance (8)
18 Money (5)
20 Up to the time when (5)
21 Darkness (5)
22 Flightless bird (3)
23 Tendency to disintegrate (11)

Down

2 Found agreeable (5)
3 Motet (anag.) (5)
4 Threaten (6)
5 Fifth Greek letter (7)
6 Sells abroad (7)
7 Two missed serves in a row (tennis) (6,5)
8 Shameful (11)
14 Male sibling (7)
15 Mercury alloy (7)
17 Roll of parchment (6)
18 SI unit of luminous flux (5)
19 Strategic board game (5)

PUZZLE 64

Across

1 Portion of medicine (4)
3 Large root vegetable (8)
9 Sculptured figures (7)
10 Muscular strength (5)
11 Data entered into a system (5)
12 Small dog (7)
13 Scrape (anag.) (6)
15 Becomes alert after sleep (6)
17 Bring an accusation against (7)
18 Sharp-pointed metal pin (5)
20 Expel from a country (5)
21 Domain (7)
22 Longing (8)
23 Average value (4)

Down

1 Characteristically (13)
2 Skin on top of the head (5)
4 Not real or genuine (6)
5 Awkward (12)
6 Form a mental picture (7)
7 US female politician (13)
8 Underground (12)
14 Powdered spice (7)
16 Unsettled; upset (6)
19 Natural elevation (5)

PUZZLE 65

Across

1 Repositories (6)
7 Vehicle with three wheels (8)
8 Court (3)
9 Spanish rice dish (6)
10 Neat in appearance (4)
11 Loosen up (5)
13 Lessen (7)
15 Gnawing animal (7)
17 Country in East Asia (5)
21 This grows on your head (4)
22 Dung beetle (6)
23 Nevertheless (3)
24 Fatherly (8)
25 Scattered about (6)

Down

1 Water diviner (6)
2 Push forward (6)
3 Motionless (5)
4 Predatory fish (7)
5 Exaggerated emotion (8)
6 Flatfish (6)
12 Of many different kinds (8)
14 Explanations (7)
16 Graphical representation of a person (6)
18 Small stone (6)
19 Make tidier (6)
20 Irritates (5)

PUZZLE 66

Across

1 Wharf (4)
3 Part of a house (8)
9 Illness (7)
10 River cove; bay (5)
11 Beam of light (3)
12 Move to music (5)
13 Sheikhdom on the Persian Gulf (5)
15 Sprites (5)
17 Pipes (5)
18 19th Greek letter (3)
19 Extent or limit (5)
20 Twist out of shape (7)
21 Scope for freedom (8)
22 Ruse (4)

Down

1 Four-sided figure (13)
2 Alleviate (5)
4 Bear witness (6)
5 Radishes grin (anag.) (12)
6 Elongated rectangles (7)
7 Where you were born (6,7)
8 Having a tendency to become liquid (12)
14 Fractional part (7)
16 Expressed something in words (6)
18 Mythical monster (5)

PUZZLE 67

Across

1 State of the USA (8)
5 A brief piece of film (4)
9 Path or road (5)
10 Slender stemlike plant appendage (7)
11 Effects or results (12)
14 Clumsy person (3)
15 Repasts (5)
16 Increase in amount (3)
17 Entirety (12)
20 Necessary (7)
22 Tree branch (5)
23 Apex or peak (4)
24 Disapproved of (8)

Down

1 Roman god of war (4)
2 Stem the flow of (4,3)
3 Omit too much detail (12)
4 Long deep track (3)
6 Expressing emotions (of poetry) (5)
7 Fence of stakes (8)
8 Untimely (12)
12 Liquid measure (5)
13 Explosively unstable (8)
16 Attack (7)
18 Confronts (5)
19 Low dull sound (4)
21 Scientific workplace (abbrev.) (3)

PUZZLE 68

Across

1 Froth of soap and water (4)
3 Relating to sound (8)
9 Envelops (7)
10 Unsteady (5)
11 Obtained (3)
12 High up (5)
13 Listens to (5)
15 Number of deadly sins (5)
17 Complete trust (5)
18 Tropical constrictor (3)
19 Daisy-like flower (5)
20 Optimistic about something (7)
21 Made less bright (8)
22 Jelly or culture medium (4)

Down

1 Legerdemain (7,2,4)
2 A finger or toe (5)
4 Trigonometric function (6)
5 Not guided by good sense (12)
6 Wealthy businesspeople (7)
7 Code-breaker (13)
8 Framework for washed garments (7,5)
14 Faster (7)
16 Feasible (6)
18 Living thing (5)

PUZZLE 69

Across

1 Intricately (11)
9 Edge of a cup (3)
10 Sense experience (5)
11 Grave and serious (5)
12 Praise enthusiastically (5)
13 Type of pasta (8)
16 Living thing (8)
18 Folded back part of a coat (5)
20 Satisfied a desire (5)
21 Microscopic fungus (5)
22 Limb used for walking (3)
23 Rude (11)

Down

2 Threshold (5)
3 Asian pepper plant (5)
4 World's largest country (6)
5 Day of the week (7)
6 Captain's record (7)
7 Glass buildings (11)
8 Phraseology (11)
14 Fact of being overly absorbed in oneself (7)
15 Capable of relieving pain (7)
17 Learned person (6)
18 Language of the Romans (5)
19 Large mast (5)

PUZZLE 70

Across

1 Devices that illuminate (6)
7 Glowing with heat (5-3)
8 Excavated soil (3)
9 Eat hurriedly (6)
10 Land measure (4)
11 Tortoise carapace (5)
13 Boastful person (7)
15 Method of presenting a play (7)
17 Long for (5)
21 Smoke passage (4)
22 Sloping (of a typeface) (6)
23 Cause friction (3)
24 Abiding; lasting (8)
25 Fast (6)

Down

1 Soup spoons (6)
2 Flock of geese (6)
3 Absorbent pads (5)
4 Move apart (7)
5 Witty reply (8)
6 Gets onto a boat (6)
12 Woody (8)
14 Rude (7)
16 Particularly strong ability (6)
18 Increase over time (6)
19 Agilely (6)
20 Sudden sharp pains (5)

PUZZLE 71

Across

1 Pertaining to the arts (8)
5 Meat from a calf (4)
9 Capital of Bulgaria (5)
10 Yield (7)
11 Constantly; always (12)
13 Meal where guests serve themselves (6)
14 Declares invalid (6)
17 Therapeutic use of plant extracts (12)
20 Snuggles (7)
21 Steer (anag.) (5)
22 Fine powder (4)
23 Type of coffee (8)

Down

1 Price (4)
2 Rise into the air (of an aircraft) (4,3)
3 Not capable of reply (12)
4 Support; help (6)
6 Break out with force (5)
7 Campaigner (8)
8 Creator of film scripts (12)
12 Got hold of (8)
15 Tennis officials (7)
16 Treatises (6)
18 Expels from a position (5)
19 Brave person; idol (4)

PUZZLE 72

Across

1 School test (4)
3 Friendly (8)
9 Type of alcohol (7)
10 Seventh sign of the zodiac (5)
11 Wander aimlessly (3)
12 In the company of (5)
13 Ball of lead (5)
15 Take place; happen (5)
17 Not straight (of hair) (5)
18 Item used in cricket (3)
19 Machine for shaping wood or metal (5)
20 Packed (7)
21 Boating (8)
22 Depend upon (4)

Down

1 Vigorously (13)
2 Hankered after (5)
4 One's environment (6)
5 Fellow plotter (12)
6 Large monkeys (7)
7 In an inflated manner (13)
8 Joblessness (12)
14 Nonconformist (7)
16 High-kicking dance (6)
18 Form of identification (5)

PUZZLE 73

Across

1 e.g. a mallard (4)
3 Obstruction in a passage (8)
9 Revive; renew (7)
10 Exposes to danger (5)
11 Practice of mentioning famous people one knows (4-8)
13 Walk with long steps (6)
15 Leguminous tree (6)
17 Grandeur (12)
20 External (5)
21 Put in someone's care (7)
22 Solidity (8)
23 Poses a question (4)

Down

1 Silliness (8)
2 Dairy product (5)
4 Type of muscle (6)
5 Shrewdness (12)
6 Poisonous metallic element (7)
7 Opposite of west (4)
8 Evergreen shrub (12)
12 Mixing boards (8)
14 Creator (anag.) (7)
16 Makes available for sale (6)
18 Words that identify things (5)
19 Bark of a dog (4)

PUZZLE 74

Across

1 Pertaining to marriage (11)
9 Timid (3)
10 Make available for sale (5)
11 Flow with a whirling motion (5)
12 Gets less difficult (5)
13 Individuality (8)
16 Utters repeatedly (8)
18 Brilliant and clear (5)
20 Passenger ship (5)
21 Form of oxygen found in the atmosphere (5)
22 Mountain pass (3)
23 Yearly celebration (11)

Down

2 Chasm (5)
3 Tree anchors (5)
4 Slightly annoyed (6)
5 Caring for (7)
6 Drug that relieves pain (7)
7 Basically (11)
8 Pamper (11)
14 Gathering of old friends (7)
15 Capital of Kenya (7)
17 Repeat performance (6)
18 Opinions (5)
19 Clergyman (5)

PUZZLE 75

Across

1 Seed containers (4)
3 Flammable liquid (8)
9 Piece of furniture (7)
10 Ancient harps (5)
11 Obfuscation (12)
14 Unit of current (3)
16 Fine powdery foodstuff (5)
17 Organ of sight (3)
18 Intolerable (12)
21 Dwelling (5)
22 Pasta strips (7)
23 War memorial (8)
24 Pairs (4)

Down

1 Pertaining to the chest (8)
2 Moneys owed (5)
4 Statute (3)
5 Repetition of the same sound (12)
6 Envisage (7)
7 Overly curious (4)
8 Inadequate (12)
12 Make right (5)
13 Turns around (8)
15 Flightless seabird (7)
19 Under (5)
20 Stylish (4)
22 Quick sleep (3)

PUZZLE 76

Across

1 Rural scenery (11)
9 School of thought (5)
10 Part of a coat (3)
11 Show indifference with the shoulders (5)
12 Sudden fear (5)
13 Evoke memories (8)
16 Barely (8)
18 Sticky (5)
21 Fortune-telling card (5)
22 Source of a metal (3)
23 Not illuminated (5)
24 Not having a written constitution (11)

Down

2 Weigh down (7)
3 Prodding with the elbow (7)
4 Rue doing something (6)
5 Impress a pattern on (5)
6 Twelve (5)
7 Explanation of an event (11)
8 Prophetic of the end of the world (11)
14 Chatter (7)
15 Go back over again (7)
17 Underground store (6)
19 Free from dirt (5)
20 Period between childhood and adulthood (5)

PUZZLE 77

Across

1 Maintenance (11)
9 Cereal grain (3)
10 Firearm (5)
11 Intimate companion (5)
12 Portion (5)
13 Brilliant performers (8)
16 Relating to time (8)
18 Elevated step (5)
20 Bright; cheery (5)
21 Doctrine; system of beliefs (5)
22 Fruit of a rose (3)
23 Lacking distinguishing characteristics (11)

Down

2 Unfasten (5)
3 Powerful forward movement (5)
4 Sightseeing trip in Africa (6)
5 Small holes in cloth or leather (7)
6 V-shaped mark (7)
7 Neutral (11)
8 Instrument for recording heart activity (11)
14 Issue forth (7)
15 Imitator (7)
17 Seem (6)
18 School of fish (5)
19 Cinders (5)

PUZZLE 78

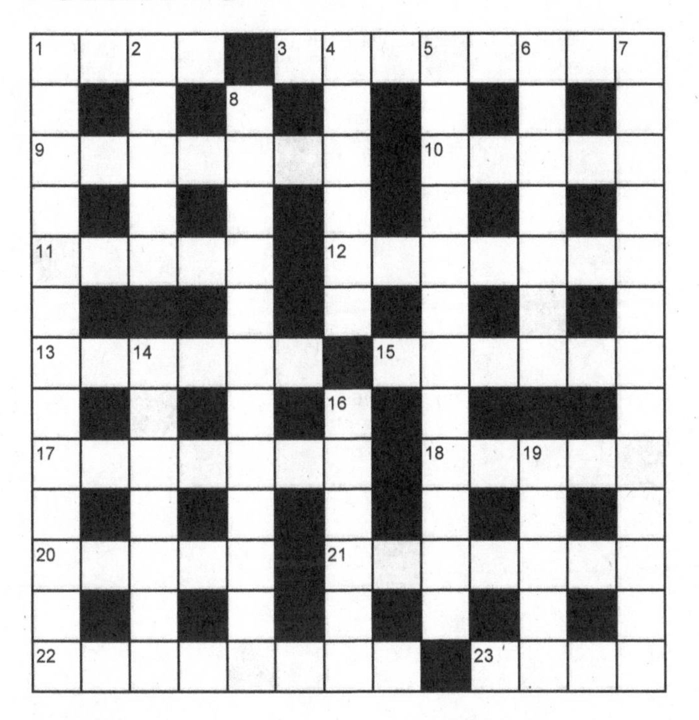

Across

1 Move fast in a straight line (4)
3 Acted with hesitation (8)
9 Country in West Africa (7)
10 Factual evidence (5)
11 Feeling of boredom (5)
12 Uncertain (7)
13 Became stuck (6)
15 Deteriorate (6)
17 Made to individual order (7)
18 One of the United Arab Emirates (5)
20 Smallest quantity (5)
21 Insignificant (7)
22 All people (8)
23 Movement of water causing a small whirlpool (4)

Down

1 25th anniversary celebration (6,7)
2 Living in a city (5)
4 Son of Daedalus in Greek mythology (6)
5 Abnormal anxiety about health (12)
6 Violent troublemakers (7)
7 In a servile manner (13)
8 Laudatory (12)
14 Communication; note (7)
16 Subatomic particle such as an electron (6)
19 Construct (5)

PUZZLE 79

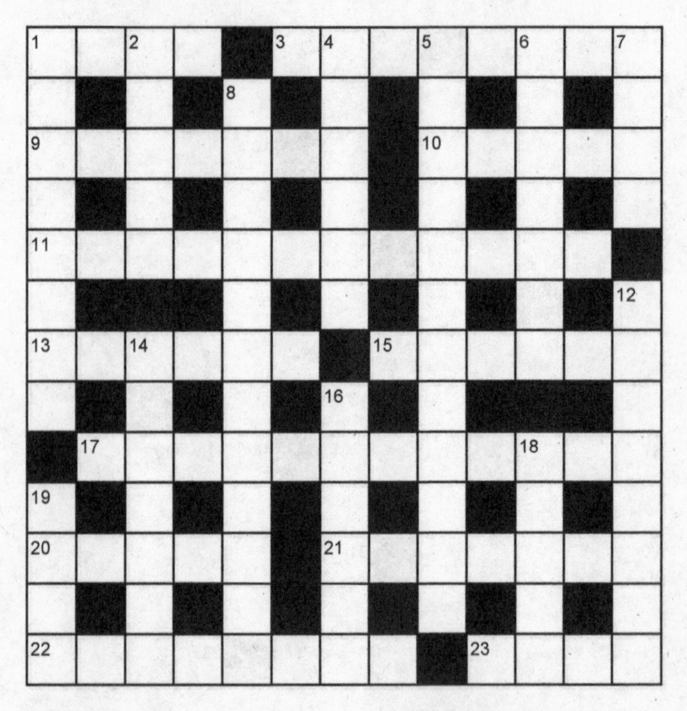

Across

1 Annoy (4)
3 Person implementing a will (8)
9 Cork for sealing a bottle (7)
10 Requirements (5)
11 Minimum purchase cost at auction (7,5)
13 Among (6)
15 Stick to (6)
17 Germicide (12)
20 Burning (5)
21 Floating mass of frozen water (7)
22 Passageway (8)
23 Paradise garden (4)

Down

1 Fail to look after properly (8)
2 Collapses (5)
4 Ancient Persian king (6)
5 Showed not to be true (12)
6 Molasses (7)
7 Rough or harsh sound (4)
8 Brutally; harshly (12)
12 Polygon with five sides (8)
14 Existing at the beginning (7)
16 Continent (6)
18 Change (5)
19 Heroic tale (4)

PUZZLE 80

Across

1 Opposite of front (4)
3 Extreme audacity (8)
9 Rotating (7)
10 Cancel (5)
11 Unfriendly (12)
14 Diving bird (3)
16 Alert (5)
17 Cook in hot oil (3)
18 Very eager; keen (12)
21 Funny person (5)
22 e.g. chlorine or bromine (7)
23 Senseless (8)
24 Skin irritation (4)

Down

1 Act of treachery (8)
2 Mark of insertion (5)
4 Domesticated pig (3)
5 Capable of being moved (12)
6 Pope (7)
7 Assist (4)
8 Pertaining to a person's life (12)
12 Approaches (5)
13 Bulbous perennial herb (8)
15 Blood relation (7)
19 Taut (5)
20 Con; swindle (4)
22 Possesses (3)

PUZZLE 81

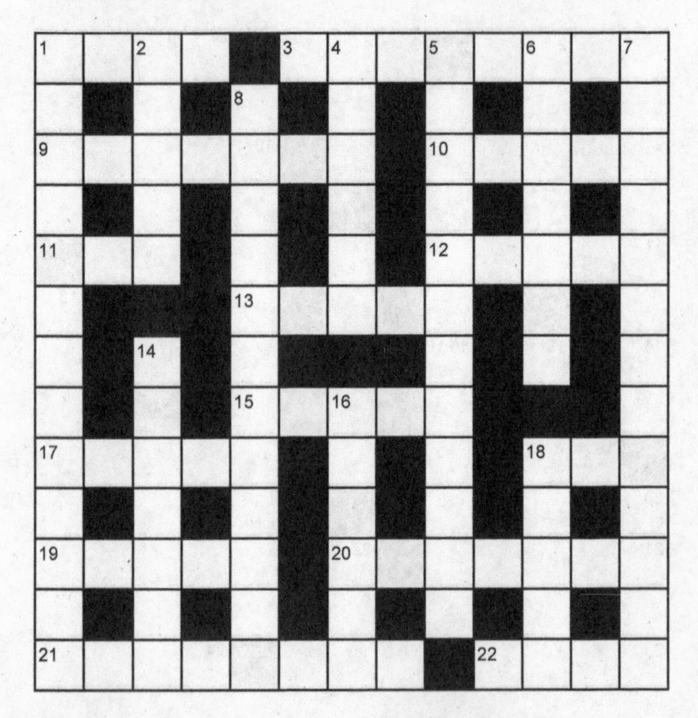

Across

1 Portfolio (4)
3 Religion (8)
9 Creatures (7)
10 Warhorse (5)
11 Small social insect (3)
12 Praise highly (5)
13 Incantation (5)
15 Recycle (5)
17 Quantitative relation (5)
18 Pasture (3)
19 Our planet (5)
20 Ancestry (7)
21 Grammatical mistake (8)
22 Protruding part of the lower jaw (4)

Down

1 Bland and dull (13)
2 Very holy person (5)
4 Uncertain (6)
5 Doubting the truth of (12)
6 Imprecise (7)
7 Large sea (13)
8 Extremely harmful (12)
14 Tallier (anag.) (7)
16 Male relatives (6)
18 Slender freshwater fish (5)

PUZZLE 82

Across

1 Dawn (8)
5 Trees of the genus Ulmus (4)
9 Underground worker (5)
10 Relating to current affairs (7)
11 Secret affair (7)
12 Programmer (5)
13 Capital of Bahrain (6)
14 Confronting and dealing with (6)
17 Giraffes have long ones (5)
19 Remnant (7)
20 Act of turning up (7)
21 Camera image (5)
22 Chinese monetary unit (4)
23 Explosive shells (8)

Down

1 Given free of charge (13)
2 Have within (7)
3 24th December (9,3)
4 Navigational instrument (6)
6 Expressed clearly (5)
7 Sanctimonious (4-9)
8 Spotless (5-3-4)
15 Freezing (3-4)
16 Give a loud shout (6)
18 About (5)

PUZZLE 83

1 2 3 4 5 6 7 8 9 10 11 12 13 14 15 16 17 18 19 20 21 22 23

Across

1 Regular (8)
5 Pinnacle (4)
9 View (5)
10 Canopies (7)
11 Bump (12)
13 Adhesive putty (6)
14 Imaginary (6)
17 Pertaining to letters (12)
20 Pushed over (7)
21 Turf out (5)
22 Monetary unit of Spain (4)
23 Safety restraint in a car (4,4)

Down

1 One more than four (4)
2 Makes certain of (7)
3 Impossible to achieve (12)
4 Close at hand (6)
6 Body of rules (5)
7 Opposite of westerly (8)
8 Inflexible (12)
12 Fortify against attack (8)
15 Elusive (7)
16 Sewing instrument (6)
18 A written document (5)
19 Proofreader's mark (4)

PUZZLE 84

1		2		3		4		■	5	6		7
	■		■		■		■	8	■		■	
9					■	10						
	■		■		■		■		■		■	
11							■	12				
	■		■		■		■		■	■	■	
13						■	14			15		
	■	■	■		■	16	■		■		■	
17		18			■	19						
	■		■		■		■		■		■	
20							■	21				
	■		■		■		■		■		■	
22				■	23							

Across

1 Card game (8)
5 Ride the waves (4)
9 Decline sharply (5)
10 Kind of whisky (7)
11 Central cell part (7)
12 Country in the Middle East (5)
13 Lasted (anag.) (6)
14 French dance (6)
17 Walks through water (5)
19 Non-specific (7)
20 Rainy season (7)
21 Ring-shaped roll (5)
22 Home for a bird (4)
23 Hand-woven pictorial design (8)

Down

1 Female professional (13)
2 A governing body in a county (7)
3 Foreboding (12)
4 Superior of a nunnery (6)
6 Brown earth pigment (5)
7 Tremendously (13)
8 Uncertain (12)
15 Standing erect (7)
16 Republic once ruled by Idi Amin (6)
18 Mounds of loose sand (5)

PUZZLE 85

Across

1 Close associate (8)
5 Matured (4)
9 Of the nose (5)
10 Slackens (7)
11 Jail term without end (4,8)
13 Narrow drinking tubes (6)
14 Loose protective garments (6)
17 Use of words that mimic sounds (12)
20 Shock physically (5-2)
21 Not asleep (5)
22 Whip (4)
23 Recreational area for children (8)

Down

1 Exposes to natural light (4)
2 Written record (7)
3 Orcas (6,6)
4 Less warm (6)
6 Obtain information from various sources (5)
7 Spread out (8)
8 Characteristic of the present (12)
12 Marriage ceremony (8)
15 The Windy City (7)
16 Force to do something (6)
18 Ellipses (5)
19 Smile broadly (4)

PUZZLE 86

Across

1 Cries (4)
3 Evading (8)
9 Periods of instruction (7)
10 Sleeveless cloaks (5)
11 Unlawful (12)
13 Make less hard (6)
15 Hawk (6)
17 Unseen observer (3,2,3,4)
20 Pointed part of a fork (5)
21 Heavy metal weights (7)
22 Cuts into bits (8)
23 Finishes (4)

Down

1 Most foolish (8)
2 Aromatic herb (5)
4 Goes to see someone (6)
5 Ineptness (12)
6 Attributed to (7)
7 Flow copiously (4)
8 Style of blues (6-6)
12 Hermits (8)
14 Pursues (7)
16 Narrow passage of water (6)
18 Decorate (5)
19 Imitated (4)

PUZZLE 87

Across

1 Scruffily (8)
5 Inspired by reverence (4)
9 Sticky sap (5)
10 Twisting; meandering (7)
11 Inventiveness (12)
14 Long and narrow inlet (3)
15 Round steering device (5)
16 Farewell remark (3)
17 Heart specialist (12)
20 Strong embrace (4,3)
22 Plant flower (5)
23 Consumes (4)
24 Ability to float (8)

Down

1 Indian dress (4)
2 European country (7)
3 Boxing class (12)
4 Opposite of high (3)
6 Forgo; relinquish (5)
7 Broke down food (8)
8 Understandably (12)
12 Model; perfect (5)
13 Vessel for molten metal (8)
16 Double-reed instrument (7)
18 Respond to (5)
19 Prestigious TV award (4)
21 Large dark antelope (3)

PUZZLE 88

Across

1 Consequently (11)
9 Plaything (3)
10 Fish-eating mammal (5)
11 Minute pore in a leaf (5)
12 Solemn promises (5)
13 Immensity (8)
16 Synthetic polymeric substances (8)
18 Noble gas (5)
20 Needing to be scratched (5)
21 Type of chemical bond (5)
22 Deep anger (3)
23 Air sport (4-7)

Down

2 Vault under a church (5)
3 Double-reed instruments (5)
4 Keep hold of (6)
5 Child's room (7)
6 Terse (7)
7 Fortified defensive position (11)
8 Unnecessarily forceful (5-6)
14 Eyelash cosmetic (7)
15 Remaining (7)
17 French fashion designer (6)
18 Competed in a speed contest (5)
19 Condescend (5)

PUZZLE 89

Across

1 Torso (4)
3 Intellectual (8)
9 Try (7)
10 Bring together (5)
11 Dispirited (12)
13 Metamorphic rock (6)
15 Botch (4-2)
17 Principal face of a building (12)
20 Raise up (5)
21 Goes back on a promise (7)
22 Took into account (8)
23 Agitate a liquid (4)

Down

1 Wave or flourish in display (8)
2 Stead (anag.) (5)
4 Confine as a prisoner (6)
5 The management of a home (12)
6 People who attack at speed (7)
7 Reasons; explanations (4)
8 Imitator (12)
12 Peacemaker (8)
14 Injuring (7)
16 Penetrate (6)
18 Number after seven (5)
19 Singe; burn (4)

PUZZLE 90

Across

1 Proclaim (8)
5 List of food options (4)
9 Trimmed (5)
10 Spanish beverage (7)
11 Loathe (5)
12 Thee (3)
13 Remote in manner (5)
15 Total disorder (5)
17 Sphere or globe (3)
19 Lazy person; layabout (5)
20 Brighten up (7)
21 Not heavy (5)
22 Affirm with confidence (4)
23 Infancy (8)

Down

1 The first and the last (5,3,5)
2 Small Arctic whale (7)
3 Perform below expectation (12)
4 Building for gambling (6)
6 Ahead of time (5)
7 Pure (13)
8 Informally (12)
14 Quick musical tempo (7)
16 Capital of Austria (6)
18 Attractive young lady (5)

PUZZLE 91

Across

1 Confuse (8)
5 Playthings (4)
8 More pleasant (5)
9 Insanitary (7)
10 Shows again (7)
12 Table support (7)
14 Sharp tooth (7)
16 Eight-sided polygon (7)
18 Final stage of a chess match (7)
19 Give a false notion of (5)
20 Appear (4)
21 Prestigious (8)

Down

1 Centre of a sail (4)
2 Casually changeable (6)
3 Managing or governing (9)
4 French museum (6)
6 Unidirectional (3-3)
7 Ominous (8)
11 Free from conflict (9)
12 General propositions (8)
13 Heavy food (6)
14 Deduces from evidence (6)
15 Type of ski race (6)
17 Sell (4)

PUZZLE 92

Across

1 Comes together; coheres (4)
3 In a friendly manner (8)
9 Makes short and sharp turns (7)
10 Pull out a hair (5)
11 Practice of designing buildings (12)
14 Sewn edge (3)
16 Customary (5)
17 Animal lair (3)
18 Swimming technique (12)
21 Capital of Vietnam (5)
22 Treated unjustly (7)
23 Scarceness (8)
24 Obstacle (4)

Down

1 Cold Spanish tomato soup (8)
2 Good sense; reasoning (5)
4 Title of a married woman (3)
5 Surrender (12)
6 Fuzzy (7)
7 Ox-like mammals (4)
8 Act of influencing someone deviously (12)
12 Show triumphant joy (5)
13 Person not expected to win (8)
15 Sailor (7)
19 Musical instrument (5)
20 Norse god of thunder (4)
22 Saw (anag.) (3)

PUZZLE 93

Across

1 Affiliation (11)
9 Foot extremity (3)
10 Captivates (5)
11 Sharp peak (5)
12 Creator (5)
13 Teaches (8)
16 Gathers in crops (8)
18 Humped ruminant (5)
20 White soft limestone (5)
21 Ironic metaphor (5)
22 Extend out (3)
23 Type of treatment using needles (11)

Down

2 Streamlined (5)
3 Opposite one of two (5)
4 Pressed clothes (6)
5 Tuft of grass (7)
6 Remove a difficulty (7)
7 Pain in a person's belly (7,4)
8 Coarse cotton gauze (11)
14 Derived from living matter (7)
15 Type of computer (7)
17 Wealthy person in business (6)
18 Fastening device (5)
19 Army rank (5)

PUZZLE 94

Across

1 Dither; excessive concern (4)
3 Spanish dance (8)
9 Former student (7)
10 Remove hair (5)
11 Cooking appliance (3)
12 Baking appliances (5)
13 Red-chested bird (5)
15 Short musical composition (5)
17 Receded (5)
18 Definite article (3)
19 Tropical fruit (5)
20 Simian (7)
21 Rocked (8)
22 Modify (4)

Down

1 Boxing class division (13)
2 Small firework (5)
4 Boards (anag.) (6)
5 Unplugged (12)
6 Most tidy (7)
7 Exaggeration (13)
8 Coming between two things (12)
14 Bright and striking (7)
16 Action of making use of something (6)
18 Bronze medal position (5)

PUZZLE 95

Across

1 Short nail (4)
3 Obscures the light from a celestial body (8)
9 Diplomatic building (7)
10 Flowering plant (5)
11 Study of microorganisms (12)
14 Finish (3)
16 Sheet (anag.) (5)
17 Bland soft food (3)
18 First part of the Bible (3,9)
21 West Indian dance (5)
22 Customs of a society (7)
23 Reserved in advance (3-5)
24 Golf pegs (4)

Down

1 Quivered (8)
2 Having three dimensions (5)
4 Bashful; reluctant to give details (3)
5 Immune (12)
6 Temporary measure (7)
7 Fraud (4)
8 Intended to attract notice (12)
12 Creative thoughts (5)
13 Totally clean (8)
15 Mark the boundaries of (7)
19 Draw or bring out (5)
20 Expression of regret (4)
22 Popular edible fish (3)

PUZZLE 96

Across

1 Calamity or great loss (11)
9 Pollex (5)
10 Silent (3)
11 Huge (5)
12 Use inefficiently; rubbish (5)
13 Superficial (4-4)
16 All-round view (8)
18 Religious table (5)
21 Flaring stars (5)
22 Female sheep (3)
23 Chefs (5)
24 Narrator (11)

Down

2 Human-like robot (7)
3 Is present at (7)
4 Small hairpiece (6)
5 U-shaped curve in a river (5)
6 Rounded protuberances on camels (5)
7 Elucidated by using an example (11)
8 Instantly (11)
14 Give advice to (7)
15 Recover (7)
17 Nearly (6)
19 Bird sound; chirp (5)
20 Happen again (5)

PUZZLE 97

Across

1 Writing fluids (4)
3 Oversight (8)
9 Cantered (7)
10 Once more (5)
11 Ancient boat (3)
12 Sharp end (5)
13 Entice to do something (5)
15 Hank of wool (5)
17 Seize firmly (5)
18 Nourished (3)
19 The Norwegian language (5)
20 Conquered by force (7)
21 Component parts (8)
22 Lazy (4)

Down

1 Inflexibility (13)
2 Small sales stand (5)
4 Average; moderate (6)
5 Having an acrid wit (5-7)
6 Meaninglessness (7)
7 Failure to be present at (13)
8 Atmospheric layer (12)
14 Open area of grassland (7)
16 Send for sale overseas (6)
18 Fader (anag.) (5)

PUZZLE 98

Across

1 Accredited diplomats (11)
9 Help (3)
10 Wound from a wasp (5)
11 Sharp blade (5)
12 Exchange of tennis strokes (5)
13 Worldwide outbreak (8)
16 Woodwind instrument (8)
18 Songbird (5)
20 Recipient of money (5)
21 Unexpected plot element (5)
22 Aggressive dog (3)
23 Brevity in expressing oneself (11)

Down

2 Scale representation (5)
3 Test or examine (5)
4 Mark of disgrace (6)
5 Break down chemically (7)
6 Horizontal underground stem (7)
7 Visible to the naked eye (11)
8 Science of farming (11)
14 West Indian musical style (7)
15 Relating to motion (7)
17 Morals (6)
18 Climbing spike (5)
19 Written agreements (5)

PUZZLE 99

Across

4 Extreme confusion (6)
7 Individual; private (8)
8 Add together (3)
9 Spiritual teacher (4)
10 Sport Andy Murray plays (6)
11 Restoration to life (7)
12 Military opponent (5)
15 Game of chance (5)
17 Diminish the worth of (7)
20 Bearlike (6)
21 Silence (4)
22 Beer container (3)
23 On the outer side (8)
24 Plump (6)

Down

1 Read with care (6)
2 Taking to be true (8)
3 In the place of (7)
4 Impossible to see round (of a bend) (5)
5 Person to whom a lease is granted (6)
6 Recollection (6)
13 Opposite of southern (8)
14 Does the same thing again (7)
15 Buyer and seller (6)
16 Type of confectionery (6)
18 Universe (6)
19 Fastened in position (5)

PUZZLE 100

Across

- **1** e.g. plaice (8)
- **5** Plant stalk (4)
- **9** Camel-like animal (5)
- **10** Food pantries (7)
- **11** Large gathering of people (5)
- **12** University teacher (3)
- **13** Individual things (5)
- **15** Long poems (5)
- **17** Bath vessel (3)
- **19** Measures duration (5)
- **20** Prophets (7)
- **21** Small tuned drum (5)
- **22** Japanese beverage (4)
- **23** Space rock (8)

Down

- **1** Congratulations (13)
- **2** Comparison (7)
- **3** Deceitfully (12)
- **4** Type of sausage (6)
- **6** Walk (5)
- **7** Misinterpreted (13)
- **8** Overwhelmingly compelling (12)
- **14** Keepsake; reminder (7)
- **16** Iridaceous plants (6)
- **18** Having nothing written on (of paper) (5)

PUZZLE 101

Across

1 Quash (6)
7 Many (8)
8 Made-up statement (3)
9 Network of rabbit burrows (6)
10 Journey (4)
11 Waterlogged area of land (5)
13 Putting away items (7)
15 Softly; not loudly (7)
17 Innate worth (5)
21 Egg-shaped (4)
22 Searching through something (6)
23 Happiness (3)
24 Drink consumed before bed (8)
25 Hinder the progress of (6)

Down

1 Rarely (6)
2 One who makes beer (6)
3 Way in (5)
4 Useful feature of a place (7)
5 Standards (8)
6 Swelling on the big toe (6)
12 Furtive (8)
14 Clergymen (7)
16 Uncover (6)
18 Situation that appears irresolvable (6)
19 Biochemical catalyst (6)
20 Leaps over a rope (5)

PUZZLE 102

Across

1 Unspecified in number (4)
3 Relating to weather (8)
9 Dark pigment in skin (7)
10 Produce eggs (5)
11 Slatted wooden box (5)
12 Accounts inspector (7)
13 Invalidate (6)
15 History play by Shakespeare (5,1)
17 Reindeer (7)
18 Come to a point (5)
20 Dramatic musical work (5)
21 Type of vermouth (7)
22 Believes tentatively (8)
23 In a good way (4)

Down

1 Partially awake (13)
2 Mediterranean island country (5)
4 Long and very narrow (6)
5 Mishap (12)
6 Farm vehicle (7)
7 Contentious (13)
8 Not having a backbone (12)
14 Strange (anag.) (7)
16 Surrender (6)
19 Main (5)

PUZZLE 103

Across

1 Daring; bold (11)
9 Craze (3)
10 e.g. Wordsworth and Keats (5)
11 Doglike mammal (5)
12 English homework assignment (5)
13 Offer of marriage (8)
16 Hideousness (8)
18 Cuban folk dance (5)
20 Titles (5)
21 Make law (5)
22 Piece of wood (3)
23 Embroidery (11)

Down

2 Extinct birds (5)
3 Not containing anything (5)
4 Move unsteadily (6)
5 Fashion anew (7)
6 Release (7)
7 Device used to increase thrust (11)
8 Trifling sum of money (5,6)
14 Quick look (7)
15 Eased in (anag.) (7)
17 Waste matter (6)
18 Imitative of the past (5)
19 Large fruit with pulpy flesh (5)

PUZZLE 104

■	1	2		3		4		5		6		■
7	■		■		■		■		■		■	8
	■		■	9					■	10		
11					■		■		■		■	
	■		■		■		■	12				
13								■	■	■	■	
	■		■		■	■	■	14	■	15	■	
	■	■	■	■	16	17						
18		19		20	■		■		■		■	
	■		■		■		■	21				
22			■	23					■		■	
	■		■		■		■		■		■	
■	24											■

Across

1 Act gloomily (anag.) (11)
9 Sudden contraction (5)
10 Level golf score (3)
11 Water lily (5)
12 Assisted (5)
13 Not long ago (8)
16 A desert in south-western Africa (8)
18 Hang in the air (5)
21 Faint southern constellation (5)
22 Illumination unit (3)
23 Craftiness (5)
24 Initiators (11)

Down

2 Framework (7)
3 Lost (7)
4 Flowering plant with a prickly stem (6)
5 Assumed proposition (5)
6 Looked at open-mouthed (5)
7 Green pigment in plants (11)
8 Having greatest importance (11)
14 Item of clothing (7)
15 Wash and iron (7)
17 Getting older (6)
19 Female fox (5)
20 Correct (5)

PUZZLE 105

Across

1 Insincere moral talk; bank (4)
3 Campaigner (8)
9 Time between events (7)
10 Relocated (5)
11 Unpleasant (12)
13 Increase in size (6)
15 Descend down a rock face (6)
17 Worldly (12)
20 Not together (5)
21 Vital content (7)
22 Stocky (8)
23 Lyric poems (4)

Down

1 Progeny (8)
2 Memos (5)
4 Very crowded (of a place) (6)
5 Sleepwalking (12)
6 Reduce the worth of (7)
7 Travel by horse (4)
8 Mathematics of triangles (12)
12 Bed covers (8)
14 Proportionately (3,4)
16 Ball-shaped object (6)
18 Adjusted the pitch of (5)
19 Route (4)

PUZZLE 106

Across

1 Tip the hat (4)
3 Upright (8)
9 African wild pig (7)
10 The entire scale (5)
11 Reticent and secretive (12)
14 Droop (3)
16 Select class (5)
17 Slippery fish (3)
18 A type of error in speech (8,4)
21 Confuse or obscure (5)
22 Japanese dish of raw fish (7)
23 Smiling contemptuously (8)
24 Highly excited (4)

Down

1 Dejected (8)
2 Refrain from (5)
4 Unit of energy (3)
5 Fellowship (12)
6 Vie (7)
7 Slot (anag.) (4)
8 Fast food item (12)
12 Small antelope (5)
13 Passing (of time) (8)
15 Tall quadruped (7)
19 Reclining (5)
20 Large wading bird (4)
22 Violate a law of God (3)

PUZZLE 107

Across

1 Show to be false (8)
5 Meat from a cow (4)
9 Humming sound (5)
10 More circular (7)
11 Oarsman (5)
12 Frying pan (3)
13 Make a search (5)
15 Confronts; deals with (5)
17 What painters create (3)
19 Small seat (5)
20 Sudden inclination to act (7)
21 Titled (5)
22 Protuberance on a plant (4)
23 Disturb (8)

Down

1 Firmness of purpose (13)
2 Excessively thin (7)
3 Regretfully (12)
4 Fierce woman (6)
6 Equip (5)
7 Prescience (13)
8 Most perfect example of a quality (12)
14 Eyelet placed in a hole (7)
16 Collapse (4,2)
18 Lukewarm (5)

PUZZLE 108

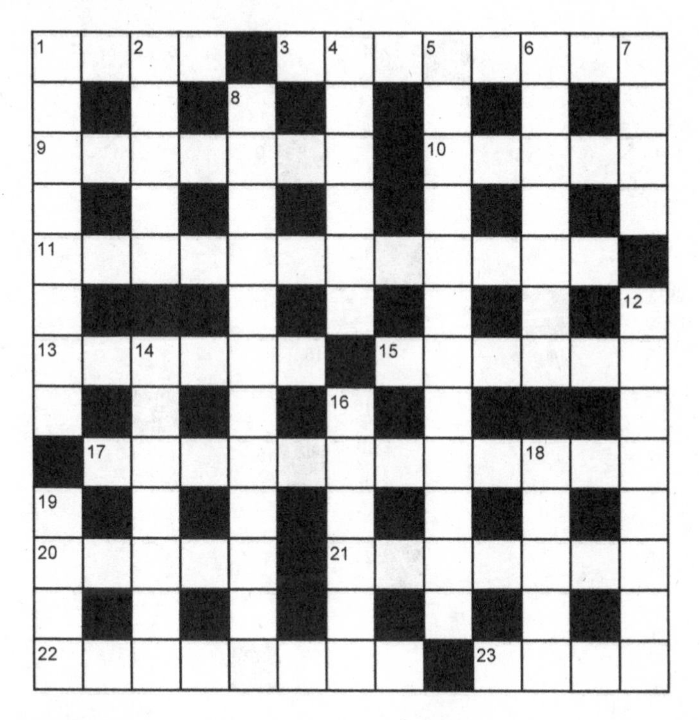

Across

1 Raised edges (4)
3 Goes before (8)
9 Virtuoso solo passage (7)
10 Pertaining to warships (5)
11 Official praise (12)
13 Removes from one's property (6)
15 Stagnation or inactivity (6)
17 Bring together into a mass (12)
20 Currently in progress (5)
21 Influences that contribute to a result (7)
22 Gloomily (8)
23 Playing cards between nines and jacks (4)

Down

1 Rebound (8)
2 Device used to connect to the internet (5)
4 Country in central Africa (6)
5 Body of voters in a given area (12)
6 Sly (7)
7 Fine soft thread (4)
8 Detective (12)
12 Judges; evaluates (8)
14 Form of an element (7)
16 Full of happiness (6)
18 Positively charged electrode (5)
19 Having little or no hair (4)

PUZZLE 109

Across

1 Sweet dessert (4)
3 Pitiful (8)
9 Massaging (7)
10 Keen (5)
11 Implant (5)
12 Works of fiction (7)
13 Lectern (6)
15 Large bottle for wine (6)
17 Nasal opening (7)
18 Hunt (5)
20 Visual representation (5)
21 Identifying outfit (7)
22 Mobster (8)
23 Position of leadership (4)

Down

1 Communicating with (13)
2 Skewered meat (5)
4 Month (6)
5 Written in pictorial symbols (12)
6 Labelling (7)
7 Plant with bright flowers (13)
8 Squint harder (anag.) (12)
14 Contempt (7)
16 Woman's garment (6)
19 Opposite of below (5)

PUZZLE 110

Across

1 Unwelcome (8)
5 Throb (4)
9 Smooth; groom (5)
10 Present (7)
11 Breathed out (7)
12 Small woody plant (5)
13 Implant deeply (6)
14 Swimming costume (6)
17 Avoided by social custom (5)
19 Great suffering (7)
20 Aperture or hole (7)
21 Egg-shaped (5)
22 Hardens (4)
23 Cut across (8)

Down

1 Not ostentatious (13)
2 If (7)
3 Not intoxicating (of a drink) (12)
4 Encrypt (6)
6 Make less miserable (5)
7 Institution (13)
8 Scolding (8-4)
15 Copy; mimic (7)
16 Occupation or profession (6)
18 Constructed (5)

PUZZLE 111

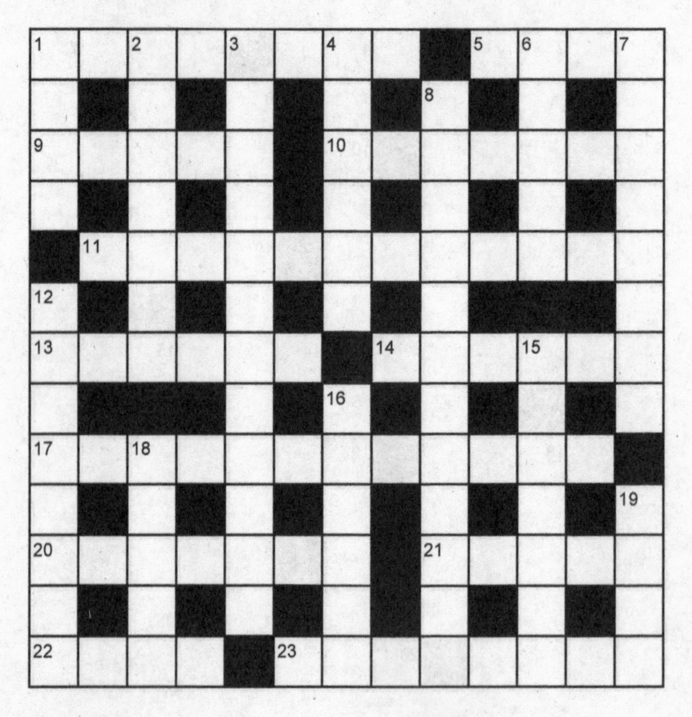

Across

1 Percussion sound (8)
5 Dice (anag.) (4)
9 Striped animal (5)
10 Public transport vehicle (7)
11 Troublemaker (6-6)
13 Boring; dull (6)
14 Musical works (6)
17 Explanatory section of a book (12)
20 Exhilarated (7)
21 African country whose capital is Niamey (5)
22 Mediocre (2-2)
23 About-face (8)

Down

1 Bewilder; stun (4)
2 Offence (7)
3 Gossip (12)
4 Worshipped (6)
6 Solids with six equal square faces (5)
7 Pain or anguish (8)
8 Ineptness (12)
12 Fans (8)
15 Aquatic invertebrates (7)
16 Nestle together (6)
18 Small nails (5)
19 Spoken test (4)

PUZZLE 112

Across

1 Chicken (4)
3 Fast runner (8)
9 Takes away (7)
10 Large woody plants (5)
11 Pay tribute to another (12)
13 Choose (6)
15 Ferocious (6)
17 Teach to accept a belief uncritically (12)
20 Parts of the cerebrum (5)
21 Friendless (7)
22 Recently married person (5-3)
23 Delighted (4)

Down

1 Predict a future event (8)
2 Ladies (5)
4 Assumes as a fact (6)
5 Comprehensible (12)
6 Small loudspeaker (7)
7 Chance taken (4)
8 In a greedy manner (12)
12 Relied on (8)
14 Archer's weapon (7)
16 Make receptive or aware (6)
18 Heavy iron tool (5)
19 Lane (anag.) (4)

PUZZLE 113

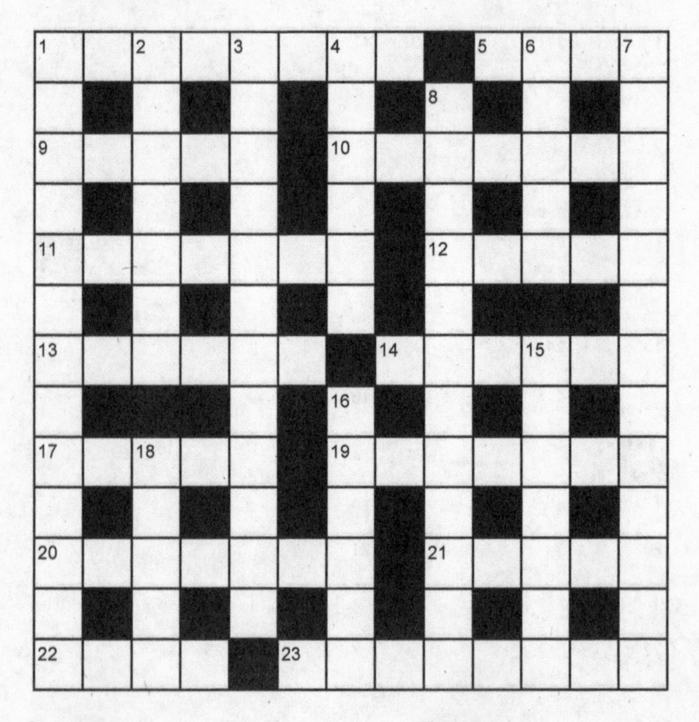

Across

1 Green vegetable (8)
5 Metallic element (4)
9 Pungent edible bulb (5)
10 Hassles; prickles (7)
11 Process of wearing away (7)
12 Mix up (5)
13 Provider of cheap accommodation (6)
14 Inside information (3-3)
17 Detailed financial assessment (5)
19 Extreme enthusiast (7)
20 Type of natural disaster (7)
21 Country once ruled by Papa Doc (5)
22 Fixed costs (4)
23 Telescope lens (8)

Down

1 Overwhelmed with sorrow (6-7)
2 Foreboding (7)
3 Private (12)
4 Protective layer (6)
6 Lazed (5)
7 Economical (4-9)
8 Connection or association (12)
15 In the fresh air (7)
16 Representation of a person (6)
18 Tennis score (5)

PUZZLE 114

Across

1 Poker stake (4)
3 Tripped (8)
9 Throb (7)
10 e.g. screwdrivers and hammers (5)
11 Drive forward (5)
12 Alfresco (4-3)
13 Cast doubt upon (6)
15 Scandinavian (6)
17 Mediocre (7)
18 What a mycologist studies (5)
20 Nationality of Oscar Wilde (5)
21 Repository (7)
22 Short film (8)
23 Wet with condensation (4)

Down

1 Increase in signal power (13)
2 Spring flower (5)
4 Vibration (6)
5 Unemotional and practical (6-2-4)
6 Garment worn by dancers (7)
7 Devastatingly (13)
8 Someone skilled in penmanship (12)
14 Trailer (7)
16 Recapture (6)
19 Sound of any kind (5)

PUZZLE 115

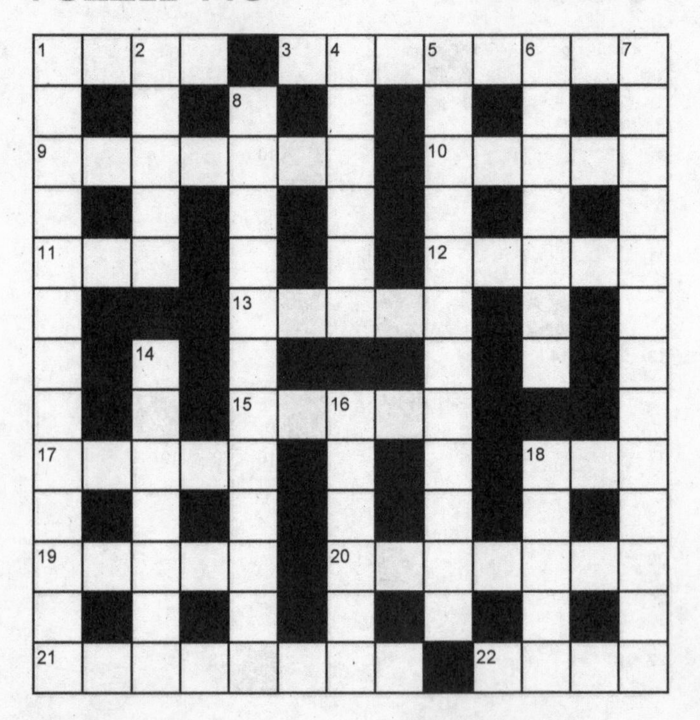

Across

1 Imperial unit (4)
3 Arithmetic operation (8)
9 Move in an exaggerated manner (7)
10 Large intestine (5)
11 Word expressing negation (3)
12 Repeat something once more (5)
13 Measuring stick (5)
15 Hold on to tightly (5)
17 Divide; separate (5)
18 Interdict (3)
19 Very masculine (5)
20 Waterproof fabric (7)
21 Solitary (8)
22 Soft cheese (4)

Down

1 Extremely small (13)
2 Hit hard (5)
4 Type of engine (6)
5 Incurably bad (12)
6 Unlawful (7)
7 Absence (13)
8 Directions (12)
14 Semiconducting element (7)
16 Impart knowledge (6)
18 One who makes bread (5)

PUZZLE 116

	1	2		3		4		5		6		
7												8
9				10								
								11				
12												
					13							
		14		15								
16						17						
								18		19		
20												
				21						22		
	23											

Across

1 Type of fat (11)
9 Blade for rowing a boat (3)
10 Not clearly stated (5)
11 Common seabirds (5)
12 Stared into space (5)
13 Increase (8)
16 Privately (8)
18 Venomous snake (5)
20 Saying; slogan (5)
21 Standpoint (5)
22 Zero (3)
23 Plant-eating insect (11)

Down

2 SI unit of frequency (5)
3 Survived (5)
4 Landmarks; spectacles (6)
5 Mournful (7)
6 Get rid of something (7)
7 US politician (11)
8 Unnecessary; superfluous (11)
14 Disperse (7)
15 Refills (7)
17 Measurement of extent (6)
18 Faint bird cry (5)
19 Spree (5)

PUZZLE 117

Across

1 Nightclub employees (8)
5 Goad on (4)
9 Play a guitar (5)
10 Stimulates; provokes (7)
11 Insincere (12)
14 Affirmative vote (3)
15 Pointed projectile (5)
16 Show discontent (3)
17 Demands or needs (12)
20 Examined hastily (7)
22 Diving waterbird (5)
23 At any time (4)
24 School pupils (8)

Down

1 Woody plant (4)
2 Second-largest European country (7)
3 Blends; mixtures (12)
4 Fish eggs (3)
6 Paved courtyard (5)
7 Electrical component (8)
8 Generally accepted (12)
12 Spiny yellow-flowered shrub (5)
13 Field game (8)
16 Among (7)
18 Tremble (5)
19 Writing instruments (4)
21 Small spot (3)

PUZZLE 118

Across

1 Reverse (4)
3 Shackle (8)
9 A placeholder name (2-3-2)
10 Less high (5)
11 Floor covering (3)
12 Variety or kind (5)
13 Compass point (5)
15 Cram (5)
17 Cruel or severe (5)
18 Be ill (3)
19 Ethos (anag.) (5)
20 Plunder (7)
21 Rubbish (8)
22 Charges (4)

Down

1 Uncaring (13)
2 Gave out playing cards (5)
4 Worshipper (6)
5 Charmingly (12)
6 Relaxes (7)
7 Absent-mindedness (13)
8 Firm rebuke (12)
14 Bodies of writing (7)
16 Ideally perfect state (6)
18 Astonish (5)

PUZZLE 119

Across

1 Employing (6)
7 Successful person (8)
8 Hair style (3)
9 Confirmed or supported a decision (6)
10 Building for grinding grain (4)
11 Polishes (5)
13 Acts in a disloyal manner (7)
15 Anxious and afraid (7)
17 Fixed platform by water (5)
21 Examine quickly (4)
22 Small cave (6)
23 Uncooked (of meat) (3)
24 Very hard carbon gems (8)
25 Tricky question (6)

Down

1 Mix socially (6)
2 Turn down (6)
3 Very strong winds (5)
4 Shake (7)
5 Damage (a reputation) (8)
6 Repeat (6)
12 e.g. Daniel or Matthew (8)
14 Pulling at (7)
16 Greek mathematician (6)
18 Decorates (6)
19 Bloom (6)
20 Brag (5)

PUZZLE 120

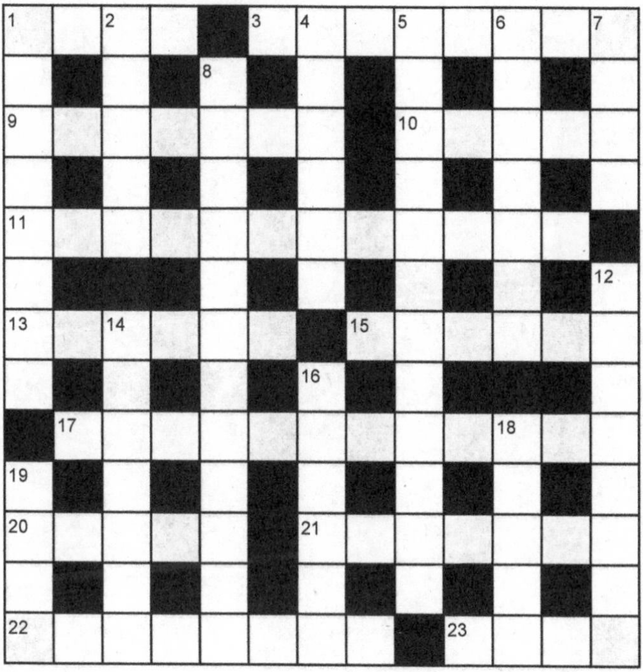

Across

1 Cloth worn around the waist (4)
3 Made still (8)
9 Volcanic crater (7)
10 Plied (anag.) (5)
11 Accomplishments (12)
13 Find (6)
15 Abscond (6)
17 Failure to act with prudence (12)
20 Finds agreeable (5)
21 Mediterranean coastal region (7)
22 Putting into practice (8)
23 Ancient harp (4)

Down

1 Friendly and outgoing (8)
2 Spirit of the air (5)
4 Overjoyed (6)
5 Uneasy (12)
6 Force of civilians trained as soldiers (7)
7 Fathers (4)
8 Incessantly (12)
12 Religious deserter (8)
14 Laugh unrestrainedly (5,2)
16 Nerve cell (6)
18 All (5)
19 Simple aquatic organism (4)

PUZZLE 121

Across

1 Inventiveness (11)
9 Bustle (3)
10 Follows orders (5)
11 Drinking tube (5)
12 Do extremely well at (5)
13 Person who supports a cause (8)
16 Doorway (8)
18 Large group of insects (5)
20 Vaulted (5)
21 Stadium (5)
22 Snare or trap (3)
23 200th anniversary of an event (11)

Down

2 Impersonator (5)
3 Evil spirit (5)
4 Required (6)
5 Scuffles (7)
6 Supervise (7)
7 Enthusiastic supporter (11)
8 Enchantment (11)
14 Things that evoke reactions (7)
15 Wound covering (7)
17 Persuasive and logical; clear (6)
18 European country (5)
19 Ire (5)

PUZZLE 122

Across

- **1** Unthinking (11)
- **9** Violent atmospheric disturbance (5)
- **10** Bun (anag.) (3)
- **11** Permit (5)
- **12** Remove wool from sheep (5)
- **13** Rush of animals (8)
- **16** Intelligentsia (8)
- **18** Tall narrow building (5)
- **21** Rough version of a document (5)
- **22** Unit of resistance (3)
- **23** Runs at a moderate pace (5)
- **24** Unintentional (11)

Down

- **2** Corridor (7)
- **3** Brushed off the face (of hair) (7)
- **4** Aquiline (6)
- **5** Unshapely masses; swellings (5)
- **6** From that time (5)
- **7** Instance of buying or selling (11)
- **8** Shortened (11)
- **14** Receiver (7)
- **15** Marmoset (7)
- **17** Call on (6)
- **19** Lady (5)
- **20** Ranked (5)

PUZZLE 123

Across

1 Church recess (4)
3 Measure of effectiveness (8)
9 Body of troops (7)
10 Drab (5)
11 Monotonously (12)
14 Support for a golf ball (3)
16 Young boy or girl (5)
17 Sprinted (3)
18 Binoculars (5,7)
21 Consumer (5)
22 Short post (7)
23 Moving at speed (8)
24 Moved quickly (4)

Down

1 Harshness of manner (8)
2 Rascal (5)
4 Facsimile (abbrev.) (3)
5 Separately (12)
6 Shaped like a ring (7)
7 Spool-like toy (4)
8 Especially (12)
12 Unspecified object (5)
13 Unequal; biased (3-5)
15 Termite (anag.) (7)
19 Pointed; acute (5)
20 Wire lattice (4)
22 Round bread roll (3)

PUZZLE 124

Across

1 Cease (4)
3 Fugitives (8)
9 Written additions (7)
10 Danger (5)
11 State of the USA (5)
12 Sour in taste (7)
13 Crazy (6)
15 Concealed from view (6)
17 Eternal (7)
18 Eighth Greek letter (5)
20 Important topic (5)
21 Widen (7)
22 The decade from 1990 - 1999 (8)
23 Walked or stepped (4)

Down

1 Accomplishment making one suitable for a job (13)
2 Country in southern Asia (5)
4 Sailor (6)
5 Gratitude (12)
6 Dressed in a vestment (7)
7 Complete in itself (of a thing) (4-9)
8 Formal notice (12)
14 Hat with a wide brim (7)
16 Functional (6)
19 Sea duck (5)

PUZZLE 125

Across

1 Consideration of the future (11)
9 Bandage that supports an arm (5)
10 Allow (3)
11 Military trainee (5)
12 Italian cathedral (5)
13 Extend beyond a surface (8)
16 Investigate (8)
18 Amphibians (5)
21 Opposite of lower (5)
22 Pot (3)
23 Make a sound expressing pain (5)
24 Science of communications in living things and machines (11)

Down

2 Located in the fresh air (7)
3 Oriental (7)
4 Applauded (6)
5 Spurred on (5)
6 Common greeting (5)
7 Producing a discordant mix of sounds (11)
8 Creating an evocative mood (11)
14 No longer in use (7)
15 Vivid (7)
17 Issue instructions; order (6)
19 Breezy (5)
20 Smooth transition (5)

PUZZLE 126

Across

1 Argues (4)
3 Wrestled (8)
9 Distant runner-up (4-3)
10 Grins (anag.) (5)
11 Author of screenplays (12)
14 Drink a little (3)
16 Musical form with a recurrent theme (5)
17 Boolean operator (3)
18 Astonishing; amazing (3-9)
21 Body of water (5)
22 Periodical (7)
23 Out of date (8)
24 Parched (4)

Down

1 Re-evaluate (8)
2 Smarter (5)
4 Flee (3)
5 Penny-pinching (12)
6 Portable lamp (7)
7 Shallow food container (4)
8 Commensurate (12)
12 Wraps closely around (5)
13 Squirmed (8)
15 Very fine substances (7)
19 Opposite of outer (5)
20 Game played on horseback (4)
22 Stream of liquid (3)

PUZZLE 127

Across

1 Impersonations (11)
9 Removed from sight (3)
10 High lending practice (5)
11 People not ordained (5)
12 Make fun of someone (5)
13 Sanitary (8)
16 Bridge above another road (8)
18 Solid blow (5)
20 Exit (5)
21 Mingle with something else (5)
22 Evergreen coniferous tree (3)
23 Tame (11)

Down

2 e.g. newspapers and TV (5)
3 Red cosmetic powder (5)
4 Sloppy (6)
5 Delightful (7)
6 Countries (7)
7 Pertaining to office workers (5-6)
8 Very tall buildings (11)
14 In reality; actually (2,5)
15 Satisfy; conciliate (7)
17 Peak (6)
18 Poisonous (5)
19 Unsuitable (5)

PUZZLE 128

Across

1 Commotion (8)
5 Capital of Norway (4)
9 Pierced by a bull's horn (5)
10 Plant-eating aquatic mammal (7)
11 Unofficially (3,3,6)
14 e.g. Hedwig in Harry Potter (3)
15 Widespread dislike (5)
16 Adult males (3)
17 Bewitchingly (12)
20 Short story (7)
22 Borough of New York City (5)
23 Anger or irritate (4)
24 Freed from captivity (8)

Down

1 Impel; spur on (4)
2 Injurious (7)
3 And also (12)
4 Goal (3)
6 Fight (3-2)
7 Exaggerated (8)
8 Unending (12)
12 Announcement (5)
13 Ruler (8)
16 Softens with age (7)
18 Polite and courteous (5)
19 Chopped; cancelled (4)
21 Wonder (3)

PUZZLE 129

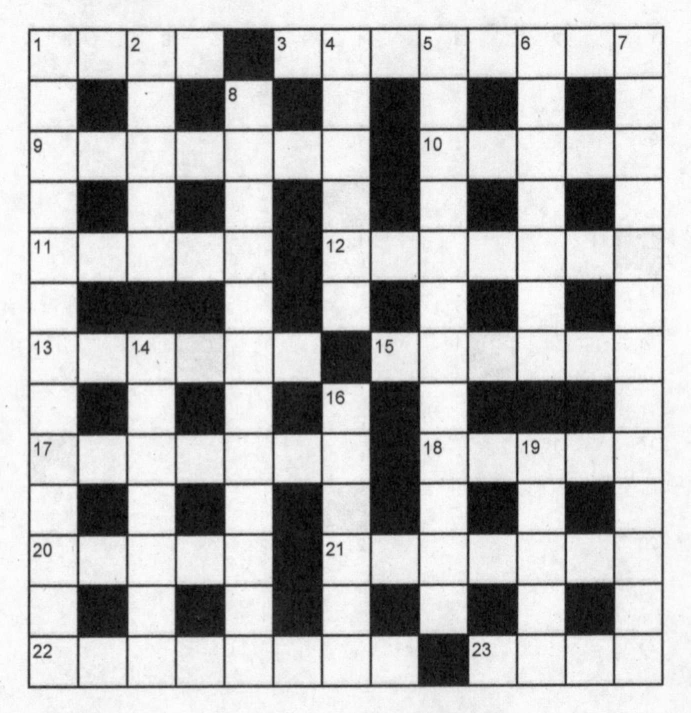

Across

1 Thick cord (4)
3 Re-emerge (8)
9 Listless (7)
10 Kingdom (5)
11 School tests (5)
12 Acknowledgement of payment (7)
13 Relaxed and informal (6)
15 Meal eaten outdoors (6)
17 Living in water (7)
18 Gain new knowledge (5)
20 Leg bone (5)
21 Provider of financial cover (7)
22 Blushed (8)
23 Effigy (4)

Down

1 Amusement park ride (6,7)
2 Mammal that eats bamboo (5)
4 Small shrubs with pithy stems (6)
5 Provincialism (12)
6 High spirits (7)
7 Device for changing TV channel (6,7)
8 Strengthen; confirm (12)
14 Rebuffed; spurned (7)
16 Opposite of passive (6)
19 Bitterly pungent (5)

PUZZLE 130

Across

1 Happen to (someone) (6)
7 Orchestral piece at the beginning of an opera (8)
8 Put down (3)
9 Chant; speak solemnly (6)
10 Hoodwink (4)
11 Enclosed (of animals) (5)
13 Sharp painful blow (7)
15 Knocking into (7)
17 Awry; lopsided (5)
21 Protest march (abbrev.) (4)
22 Gossip (6)
23 Breed of dog (3)
24 Allocated (8)
25 The rear parts of ships (6)

Down

1 Sea in northern Europe (6)
2 Cooking in hot oil (6)
3 Company emblems (5)
4 Returns to a former state (7)
5 Engravings (8)
6 Make (6)
12 Elation (8)
14 Combining (7)
16 Anxious (6)
18 Guardian (6)
19 Jams tight (6)
20 Large-headed nails (5)

PUZZLE 131

Across

1 Testimony (11)
9 Animal doctor (3)
10 Alphabetical list (5)
11 e.g. incisors and molars (5)
12 Smells strongly (5)
13 Remote; cut off (8)
16 Bald (8)
18 Principle or belief (5)
20 Choose through voting (5)
21 Command (5)
22 How (anag.) (3)
23 Clay pottery (11)

Down

2 Name of a book (5)
3 Modifies (5)
4 Makes spick and span (6)
5 Fabric (7)
6 Opposes (7)
7 Do better than expected (11)
8 Result of a person losing a lot of water (11)
14 Difficult choice (7)
15 As fast as possible (4,3)
17 Smear or blur (6)
18 Hurled away (5)
19 More recent (5)

PUZZLE 132

Across

1 Larva of a butterfly (11)
9 Lives (anag.) (5)
10 Bleat of a sheep (3)
11 Bring into a line (5)
12 Manner of speaking (5)
13 Mammal that chews the cud (8)
16 Not obligatory (8)
18 Shows tiredness (5)
21 Food relish (5)
22 Louse egg (3)
23 Decrease; lessen (5)
24 Questioning a statement (11)

Down

2 States as a fact (7)
3 Latter part of the day (7)
4 Toxin (6)
5 Misplaces (5)
6 Monastery church (5)
7 Person who foresees the future (11)
8 Fictional (4-7)
14 Perennial plant with fleshy roots (7)
15 Pancreatic hormone (7)
17 Saying (6)
19 Sorceress (5)
20 Stable compartment (5)

PUZZLE 133

Across

1 Ingredient in vegetarian cooking (4)
3 Pulled (a muscle) (8)
9 Set apart (7)
10 Borders (5)
11 Type of shelf (5)
12 Needleworker (7)
13 No one (6)
15 Comes up (6)
17 Uncovers; reveals (7)
18 Musical times (5)
20 Wireless (5)
21 Making less hot (7)
22 Reassured (8)
23 Remain in the same place (4)

Down

1 Simple problem-solving method (5,3,5)
2 Leaf of a fern (5)
4 Pinches sharply (6)
5 Improvement in a condition (12)
6 Makes ineffective (7)
7 Upsettingly (13)
8 Children's toy (12)
14 Having two feet (7)
16 The spirit or soul (6)
19 Damp (5)

PUZZLE 134

Across

1 Small pieces; bits (8)
5 Double-reed instrument (4)
9 Escapade (5)
10 Lock of curly hair (7)
11 Medicine taken when blocked-up (12)
14 Your (poetic) (3)
15 Spiritual nourishment (5)
16 Consumed food (3)
17 Having an efficient approach to one's work (12)
20 Fish-eating birds of prey (7)
22 Uproarious party or fight (5)
23 Standard (4)
24 Aromatic shrub (8)

Down

1 Religious group (4)
2 Irreverence (7)
3 Renditions (12)
4 Hill (3)
6 Strong lightweight wood (5)
7 Gives a right to (8)
8 Impregnable (12)
12 Groups of criminals (5)
13 Resolute; obstinate (8)
16 Causing difficulty (7)
18 Fantastic (5)
19 Speak indistinctly (4)
21 Expanse of salt water (3)

PUZZLE 135

Across

1 Unsure where one is (4)
3 Type of state (8)
9 Coal miner (7)
10 Scowl (5)
11 Era (anag.) (3)
12 With speed (5)
13 Not concealed (5)
15 Awaken (5)
17 Swagger (5)
18 17th Greek letter (3)
19 Brief appearance in a film by someone famous (5)
20 Junction between nerve cells (7)
21 Secret relationships (8)
22 Pottery material (4)

Down

1 Lazy (13)
2 Medicinal ointment (5)
4 Infuriate (6)
5 Uncomplimentary (12)
6 Large spotted cat (7)
7 Sweets (13)
8 Ill-mannered (12)
14 Musical instrument (7)
16 Agreement or concord (6)
18 Push away (5)

PUZZLE 136

Across

1 Look at amorously (4)
3 Fierce contest (8)
9 Hearing range (7)
10 Produce as a fruit (5)
11 Completeness (12)
13 Margin of safety (6)
15 Stage whispers (6)
17 Corresponding; proportionate (12)
20 Group of witches (5)
21 Voted in to office (7)
22 Give entirely to a cause (8)
23 Push; poke (4)

Down

1 Protective garments (8)
2 Lingers furtively (5)
4 Groups of eight (6)
5 UFO (6,6)
6 Decided based on little evidence (7)
7 Periodic movement of the sea (4)
8 Devoted to music (12)
12 Climbed (8)
14 Changed gradually over time (7)
16 Force fluid into (6)
18 Change (5)
19 Corrosive substance (4)

PUZZLE 137

Across

1 Not extreme (8)
5 Short tail (4)
9 Steep bank or slope (5)
10 Flowering shrubs (7)
11 Section of a long poem (5)
12 Cereal plant (3)
13 Research deeply (5)
15 Latin American dance (5)
17 Opposite of cold (3)
19 Timber framework (5)
20 Get better (7)
21 Selected (5)
22 Soft drink (US) (4)
23 Course of study (8)

Down

1 Party game (7,6)
2 Dandier (anag.) (7)
3 Duplication (12)
4 Go from one place to another (6)
6 Pellucid (5)
7 Blandness (13)
8 Relating to numbers (12)
14 SI unit of electric charge (7)
16 Pleasantly (6)
18 Used a computer keyboard (5)

PUZZLE 138

Across

1 Brass instrument (4)
3 Roughly rectangular (8)
9 State freely (7)
10 These keep your feet warm (5)
11 In accordance with general custom (12)
13 Instrumental piece of music (6)
15 Official proclamations (6)
17 Resolvable (12)
20 Divide in two (5)
21 Books of maps (7)
22 Base of a statue (8)
23 Hind part (4)

Down

1 Always in a similar role (of an actor) (8)
2 Moved by air (5)
4 Surprise results (6)
5 Inharmoniously (12)
6 Antiquated (7)
7 Freedom from difficulty or hardship (4)
8 Notwithstanding (12)
12 Evaluator (8)
14 Provoked or teased (7)
16 Leaping antelope (6)
18 Moisten meat (5)
19 Vessel (4)

PUZZLE 139

Across

4 Scuffle (6)
7 Sharp heel (8)
8 Ate (anag.) (3)
9 Country in West Africa (4)
10 Intense beams of light (6)
11 Strangeness (7)
12 Flightless birds (5)
15 Strong cords (5)
17 Spread out (7)
20 Feeling a continuous dull pain (6)
21 Engrossed (4)
22 Be nosy (3)
23 Something in the way (8)
24 Make beloved (6)

Down

1 Drive aground (a boat) (6)
2 Association created for mutual benefit (8)
3 Chic (7)
4 Browned bread (5)
5 Playground structure (6)
6 Avoids (6)
13 Very annoying (8)
14 Largest (7)
15 Small wave (6)
16 Took part in a game (6)
18 Flexible (6)
19 Lesser (5)

PUZZLE 140

Across

1 Images recorded on film (11)
9 Australian marsupial (5)
10 Marry (3)
11 Russian spirit (5)
12 Craftsman who uses stone (5)
13 Dawdlers (8)
16 Country in Africa (8)
18 Levels; ranks (5)
21 Corpulent (5)
22 Lyric poem (3)
23 Single-celled plants (5)
24 Pretentious display (11)

Down

2 Sausages in bread rolls (3,4)
3 Fusion chamber (7)
4 Looked at menacingly (6)
5 Warning sound (5)
6 Screams (5)
7 Reduction in worth (11)
8 Forever (2,9)
14 Sweet course (7)
15 Capital of Ontario (7)
17 Get off (6)
19 Seven (anag.) (5)
20 Tremble (5)

PUZZLE 141

Across

1 Created (4)
3 Migratory birds (8)
9 Featured in the leading role (7)
10 Animal that uses two legs for walking (5)
11 Female school boss (12)
14 Short cylindrical piece of wood (3)
16 Wander aimlessly (5)
17 Intentionally so written (3)
18 Place of conflict (12)
21 Robbery (5)
22 Sum added to interest (7)
23 Lack of flexibility (8)
24 Sixth Greek letter (4)

Down

1 Emphasis (anag.) (8)
2 Stage play (5)
4 Roll of bank notes (3)
5 Scientific research rooms (12)
6 Argues against (7)
7 Team (4)
8 Planned in advance (12)
12 Desire to hurt someone (5)
13 The scholastic world (8)
15 Eating grass (of cattle) (7)
19 Join together (5)
20 US pop star who sang I Got You Babe (4)
22 Place (3)

PUZZLE 142

	1	2		3		4		5		6		
7												8
9				10								
								11				
12												
					13							
		14		15								
16						17						
								18		19		
20												
				21						22		
	23											

Across

1 Meat-eating (11)
9 Mist (3)
10 Gold block (5)
11 Informs (5)
12 Mountainous (5)
13 Mesmerism (8)
16 Sleep disorder (8)
18 Worthiness (5)
20 Armistice (5)
21 Broadcast again (5)
22 Ignited (3)
23 Youth (11)

Down

2 Attendant upon God (5)
3 Very loud (5)
4 Quirk (6)
5 Decaying (7)
6 Unfasten (7)
7 Where one finds Kabul (11)
8 Revive (11)
14 Confident (7)
15 Endanger (7)
17 Insure (anag.) (6)
18 Chop meat into very small pieces (5)
19 Ancient object (5)

PUZZLE 143

Across

4 Treeless Arctic region (6)
7 Substantial (8)
8 Home for a pig (3)
9 Closing section of music (4)
10 Fighting between armed forces (6)
11 Mandible (7)
12 Cover with liquid (5)
15 Managed (5)
17 Newness (7)
20 Matter (6)
21 Eager; keen (4)
22 Fellow (3)
23 Distinction; high status (8)
24 Immature of its kind (of insects) (6)

Down

1 Gaseous envelope of the sun (6)
2 Clamber (8)
3 Discourse on a theme (7)
4 Conditions (5)
5 Rusted (anag.) (6)
6 Regardless (6)
13 Portents (8)
14 Desist from (7)
15 Club (6)
16 Request made to God (6)
18 Settle decisively (6)
19 A central point (5)

PUZZLE 144

Across

1 With undiminished force (8)
5 Mineral powder (4)
9 Triangular river mouth (5)
10 Impresario (7)
11 Lively festivities (7)
12 Prod with the elbow (5)
13 Pulsates (6)
14 Leave (6)
17 Country in the Himalayas (5)
19 Got away (7)
20 Provokes (7)
21 Consent to (5)
22 Award (informal) (4)
23 Complains (8)

Down

1 Comprehension (13)
2 Finished (3,4)
3 Quality of being at hand when necessary (12)
4 Pieces of writing (6)
6 Targeted (5)
7 Satisfaction (13)
8 Comical tuner (anag.) (12)
15 Clothing (7)
16 Moral guardian (6)
18 Brown nut (5)

PUZZLE 145

Across

1 Transfer responsibility elsewhere (4,3,4)
9 Signal assent with the head (3)
10 Pertaining to the ear (5)
11 Long-legged bird (5)
12 Voting compartment (5)
13 Area of the zodiac (4,4)
16 Retort (8)
18 Lobed glandular organ (5)
20 Severe (5)
21 Japanese mattress (5)
22 Cheek (slang) (3)
23 Giant aerial (anag.) (11)

Down

2 Relating to sound (5)
3 Make a long narrow gash (5)
4 Large wasp (6)
5 Defensive wall (7)
6 Pipe (7)
7 Inattentive (11)
8 Accurate timer (11)
14 Distributing (7)
15 Mournful (7)
17 Group of seven (6)
18 Of the moon (5)
19 Roman country house (5)

PUZZLE 146

Across

1 Fish appendages (4)
3 Tepid (8)
9 Varnish (7)
10 Top degree mark (5)
11 Corpulent (5)
12 Spouse (7)
13 Royal chair (6)
15 Former female pupil (6)
17 Earthquake scale (7)
18 Japanese dish (5)
20 Speak (5)
21 Guilty person (7)
22 Powerless (8)
23 Heroic poem (4)

Down

1 Continue a stroke in tennis (6,7)
2 Mother-of-pearl (5)
4 Not ready to eat (of fruit) (6)
5 Easily (12)
6 Kind of abbreviation (7)
7 Desiring worldly possessions (13)
8 Occult (12)
14 Musical performance (7)
16 Follows the position of (6)
19 Remove paint from a wall (5)

PUZZLE 147

Across

1 Took military action against (8)
5 High-value playing cards (4)
9 In a slow tempo (of music) (5)
10 Obstruction (7)
11 Room attached to a house (12)
13 Top quality (6)
14 Selected (6)
17 Immeasurably (12)
20 Information (7)
21 Epic poem ascribed to Homer (5)
22 Run quickly (4)
23 To some degree (8)

Down

1 Associate (4)
2 Tumult (7)
3 Question in great detail (5-7)
4 Set out on a journey (6)
6 Coarse twilled cotton fabric (5)
7 Splashing with water (8)
8 Awe-inspiring (12)
12 Confessed to be the case (8)
15 Unaccompanied musician (7)
16 Adornment of hanging threads (6)
18 Ciphers (5)
19 Anxious; nervous (4)

PUZZLE 148

Across

1 State of preoccupation (11)
9 Edible nut (3)
10 Not tense (5)
11 Cowboy exhibition (5)
12 Unfasten a garment (5)
13 Most pleased (8)
16 Measure of the heat content of a system (8)
18 Snake (5)
20 Porcelain (5)
21 Enthusiasm (5)
22 Hog (3)
23 Company that transmits TV shows (11)

Down

2 Type of jazz (5)
3 Bird claw (5)
4 Single-celled organism (6)
5 Type of treatment for a disorder (7)
6 Exceeds; surpasses (7)
7 Happenings (11)
8 Cheat someone financially (5-6)
14 Stirred (anag.) (7)
15 Capital of Nicaragua (7)
17 Unit of astronomical length (6)
18 Natural satellites (5)
19 Acer tree (5)

PUZZLE 149

Across

1 Wisdom (8)
5 A person's individuality (4)
9 Snake toxin (5)
10 Cold-blooded vertebrate like a crocodile (7)
11 Showed (12)
13 Relations by marriage (2-4)
14 Frightens (6)
17 Unkind; unsympathetic (12)
20 Disciple (7)
21 State indirectly (5)
22 Pitcher (4)
23 Come before in time (8)

Down

1 Salvage (4)
2 Respectable; refined (7)
3 A grouping of states (12)
4 Songbird with a spotted breast (6)
6 Be alive; be real (5)
7 Diabolically cruel (8)
8 Showing gratitude (12)
12 Imitate (8)
15 Fall back (7)
16 Common bird (6)
18 Aromatic spice (5)
19 Sort (4)

PUZZLE 150

1		2		■	3	4		5		6		7
	■		■	8	■		■		■		■	
9							■	10				
	■		■		■		■		■		■	
11					■	12						
	■	■	■		■		■		■		■	
13		14				■	15					
	■		■		■	16	■		■	■	■	
17							■	18		19		
	■		■		■		■		■		■	
20					■	21						
	■		■		■		■		■		■	
22								■	23			

Across

1 Part of the eye (4)
3 Beast with three heads (8)
9 Piece of art made from various materials (7)
10 Exceed (5)
11 Crazy (5)
12 Three-pronged weapon (7)
13 Make worse (6)
15 Having been defeated (6)
17 Unpredictable (7)
18 Group of shots (5)
20 Excuse of any kind (5)
21 Correspondence (7)
22 Supplication (8)
23 Catch sight of (4)

Down

1 Thoughtless (13)
2 Tiles (anag.) (5)
4 Votes into office (6)
5 Variety of wildlife in an area (12)
6 Backtrack (7)
7 Impulsively (13)
8 Intricate and confusing (12)
14 Carry on (7)
16 Wildcat (6)
19 Looks slyly (5)

PUZZLE 151

Across

1 Obstacle; barrier (11)
9 Absolutely (3)
10 Computer memory units (5)
11 Speaks (5)
12 Study (anag.) (5)
13 Keep at a distance (8)
16 Enticing (8)
18 Hold responsible (5)
20 One image within another (5)
21 Peers (5)
22 Head covering (3)
23 Fragility (11)

Down

2 Starting point (5)
3 Domestic cat (5)
4 Undoes (6)
5 Food samplers (7)
6 Silhouette (7)
7 Act of publishing in several places (11)
8 Insults (11)
14 Make someone agitated (7)
15 Object strongly (7)
17 Pertaining to a nerve (6)
18 Subatomic particle (5)
19 Yearns for (5)

PUZZLE 152

Across

- **4** European flatfish (6)
- **7** An opening (8)
- **8** 24-hour period (3)
- **9** Restrain (4)
- **10** Part of a dress (6)
- **11** Kitchen implement (7)
- **12** Jests (5)
- **15** Object on which a bird roosts (5)
- **17** Delivers on a promise (7)
- **20** Showed around (6)
- **21** Posterior (4)
- **22** Witch (3)
- **23** Conclusions (8)
- **24** Marsh plants (6)

Down

- **1** Support (6)
- **2** Frenzied (8)
- **3** Argue (7)
- **4** Looks after (5)
- **5** Decorate (6)
- **6** Lymphoid organ (6)
- **13** Subsidiary (8)
- **14** Experts (7)
- **15** Shoves (6)
- **16** Tattered (6)
- **18** Touched down (6)
- **19** Goodbye (Spanish) (5)

PUZZLE 153

Across

1 Curved shape (4)
3 Public and formal (8)
9 Strong-smelling fungus (7)
10 Manages (5)
11 Next (12)
14 Tear (3)
16 Record on tape (5)
17 Conciliatory gift (3)
18 Resistant to change (12)
21 Two times (5)
22 The Netherlands (7)
23 Settling for rest (of birds) (8)
24 Metal fastener (4)

Down

1 Creative skill (8)
2 Tiny piece of food (5)
4 Sum charged (3)
5 Heartbroken (12)
6 Pierces with something sharp (7)
7 Not as much (4)
8 Bubbling (12)
12 Beneath (5)
13 Magnificent (8)
15 Stipulation (7)
19 Not suitable (5)
20 Heavenly body (4)
22 Female chicken (3)

PUZZLE 154

Across

1 Cutlery used to stir a drink (8)
5 Crush with a sharp blow (4)
9 Clean spiritually (5)
10 Horizontal supporting beams (7)
11 Lowest possible temperature (8,4)
14 Young newt (3)
15 Removes moisture (5)
16 Kind or sort (3)
17 Science of deciphering codes (12)
20 Pointless (7)
22 Comic dramatic work (5)
23 Girl or young woman (4)
24 Feud (8)

Down

1 Knocks lightly (4)
2 Performer of gymnastic feats (7)
3 Prerequisite (12)
4 Lubricate (3)
6 In what place (5)
7 Grassy clumps (8)
8 Inadequately manned (12)
12 Exploiting unfairly (5)
13 Compassionate (8)
16 Acquire from a relative (7)
18 Abominable snowmen (5)
19 Bate (anag.) (4)
21 That vessel (3)

PUZZLE 155

Across

1 Forebear (8)
5 Days before major events (4)
9 Student (5)
10 Position on top of (7)
11 Starting points (7)
12 Pattern (5)
13 Cause to start burning (6)
14 Respiratory condition (6)
17 Natural yellow resin (5)
19 Contrary to (7)
20 Signs up (7)
21 Follow on from (5)
22 Open the mouth wide when tired (4)
23 Feigns (8)

Down

1 Roughly (13)
2 Text accompanying a cartoon (7)
3 Narcissism (4-8)
4 Musician playing a double-reed instrument (6)
6 One-way flow structure (5)
7 Loyalty in the face of trouble (13)
8 Second part of the Bible (3,9)
15 Involving active participation (5-2)
16 Title of Roman emperors (6)
18 Local authority rule (2-3)

PUZZLE 156

	1	2		3		4		5		6		
7												8
				9						10		
11												
								12				
13												
								14		15		
					16	17						
18		19		20								
								21				
22				23								
	24											

Across

1 Study of lawbreaking (11)
9 Person who flies an aircraft (5)
10 Animal enclosure (3)
11 Device used to sharpen razors (5)
12 Ascended (5)
13 Regnant (8)
16 Until now (8)
18 Agree or correspond (5)
21 Roman cloaks (5)
22 Opposite of in (3)
23 Small boat (5)
24 Dividing line (11)

Down

2 Learn new skills (7)
3 Soaking up (7)
4 Wrestling hold (6)
5 Coming after (5)
6 Stares with the mouth wide open (5)
7 Direction (11)
8 Without giving a name (11)
14 Palest (7)
15 Perennial herb (7)
17 Symbolic (6)
19 Supple (5)
20 Woody-stemmed plant (5)

PUZZLE 157

Across

1 Hitting repeatedly (8)
5 Fill or satiate (4)
8 Precipitates (5)
9 Bring to life (7)
10 Restrained (7)
12 Restlessness; state of worry (7)
14 Wearing away (7)
16 Brought to bear (7)
18 Graceful in form (7)
19 Commerce (5)
20 Portent (4)
21 Mileage tracker (8)

Down

1 Country in South America (4)
2 For men and women (of clothing) (6)
3 Harm the reputation of (9)
4 Almost (6)
6 Hate (6)
7 Giving way under pressure (8)
11 Botanical garden for trees (9)
12 Secondary personality (5,3)
13 Tranquil (6)
14 Amended (6)
15 Whole (6)
17 Cry of derision (4)

PUZZLE 158

Across

1 Unskilled; amateur (8)
5 Greek god of war (4)
9 Reproach (5)
10 Assistant; follower (7)
11 Ugly thing (7)
12 Lump or bump (5)
13 Messy (6)
14 Altitude (6)
17 Academy Award (5)
19 Coincide partially (7)
20 Data input device (7)
21 Sweet-scented shrub (5)
22 Three feet (4)
23 Form of carbon (8)

Down

1 In a disbelieving manner (13)
2 Obvious (7)
3 Surpassing in influence (12)
4 Cried out (of a lion) (6)
6 Regal (5)
7 Lacking originality (13)
8 Deceiver (6-6)
15 Famous Italian astronomer (7)
16 Next after third (6)
18 Seat of authority (5)

PUZZLE 159

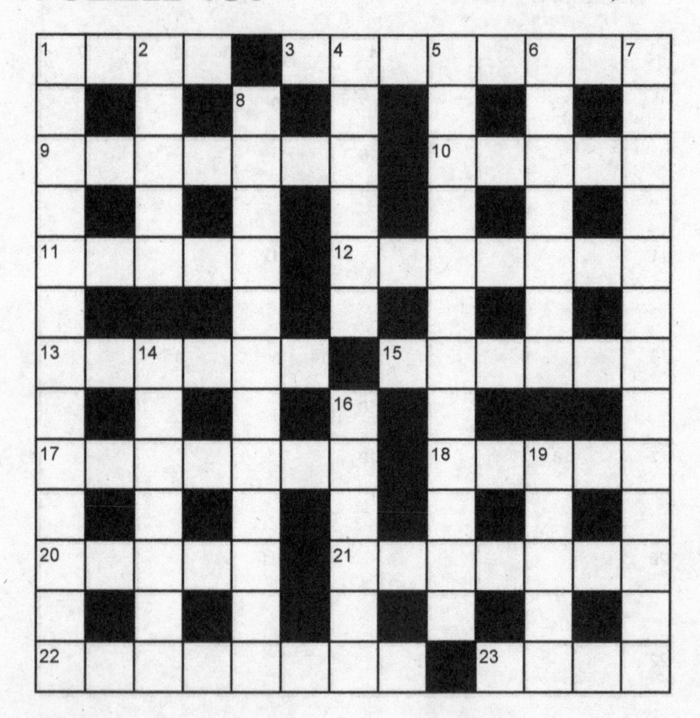

Across

1 Every (4)
3 Musical pieces for solo instruments (8)
9 Small flute (7)
10 Spring flower (5)
11 Avoid (5)
12 Feeling of aversion (7)
13 Country in North Europe (6)
15 Browns bread (6)
17 Against (7)
18 Tortilla topped with cheese (5)
20 Lacking meaning (5)
21 Stations at the ends of routes (7)
22 The priesthood (8)
23 Group of players; side (4)

Down

1 Art movement (13)
2 Chocolate powder (5)
4 Egg-shaped solids (6)
5 Long athletics race (5-7)
6 Exchanges of several strokes in tennis (7)
7 Style of painting (13)
8 Despair (12)
14 Give reasons for (7)
16 The boss at a newspaper (6)
19 Culinary herb (5)

PUZZLE 160

Across

1 Difficult choices (8)
5 Low dam across a river (4)
8 Equipped (5)
9 Plunder (7)
10 Requiring (7)
12 Beating (7)
14 Friendly (7)
16 Garments worn by women (7)
18 Wicked look that causes harm (4,3)
19 Express gratitude (5)
20 Hindu spiritual discipline (4)
21 Giant ocean waves (8)

Down

1 Clock face (4)
2 Extremes (6)
3 Drugs used to treat diseases (9)
4 Assisting (6)
6 Excitingly strange (6)
7 Demote (8)
11 Illuminate (9)
12 Swollen with fat (8)
13 Fist fighting (6)
14 Plus points (6)
15 Pacify (6)
17 Seek (anag.) (4)

PUZZLE 161

Across

1 Adequacy (11)
9 Dry (of wine) (3)
10 Ascend (5)
11 Send someone to a medical specialist (5)
12 Regions (5)
13 Open resistance (8)
16 Utopian (8)
18 Display freely (5)
20 These protect you from rain (5)
21 Instruct (5)
22 Pair of actors (3)
23 Crises (11)

Down

2 Male relation (5)
3 Concentrate on (5)
4 Cower; recoil (6)
5 Entangle (7)
6 Restrict (7)
7 Founded (11)
8 Flower (6-2-3)
14 Dignified conduct (7)
15 Close group (7)
17 Plant with oil rich seeds (6)
18 Set of moral principles (5)
19 Unwarranted (5)

PUZZLE 162

Across

4 Offered goods for sale (6)
7 Poisonous green gas (8)
8 Part of a pen (3)
9 Ballot choice (4)
10 Wishing for (6)
11 Livid (7)
12 Throw (5)
15 Penned (5)
17 Small villages (7)
20 Small insect (6)
21 Fluent but shallow (of words) (4)
22 Animal fodder (3)
23 Read out loud (8)
24 Foot levers (6)

Down

1 Easy victory (4-2)
2 Formal agreement (8)
3 Pugilist (7)
4 Piles (5)
5 Martial art (4,2)
6 Expose as being false (6)
13 Flat image that looks 3D (8)
14 Gaunt (7)
15 Do the dishes (4-2)
16 Complied with orders (6)
18 Followed closely (6)
19 Long-necked birds (5)

PUZZLE 163

Across

1 Intrinsically (8)
5 Hired form of transport (4)
9 Uncertainty (5)
10 Wavering effect in a musical tone (7)
11 Parchment rolls (7)
12 Neck warmer (5)
13 Recount (6)
14 Establish by law (6)
17 Tribe (anag.) (5)
19 Kettledrums (7)
20 Bison (7)
21 Foolishly credulous (5)
22 Otherwise (4)
23 Gusty (8)

Down

1 Incapable of being expressed in words (13)
2 Impartial (7)
3 Dictatorial (12)
4 Most recent (6)
6 Hawaiian greeting (5)
7 Harmlessly (13)
8 Calculations of dimensions (12)
15 Greed (7)
16 Walk casually (6)
18 Bunches (5)

PUZZLE 164

Across

- **4** Stifle (anag.) (6)
- **7** Repress (8)
- **8** Listening device (3)
- **9** Bone of the forearm (4)
- **10** Standard; usual (6)
- **11** Written language for blind people (7)
- **12** Walks awkwardly (5)
- **15** Small house (5)
- **17** Metal projectiles (7)
- **20** Detestable (6)
- **21** Dispatched (4)
- **22** Throat of a voracious animal (3)
- **23** Words representing numbers (8)
- **24** e.g. using a towel (6)

Down

- **1** Bank employee (6)
- **2** Robbing (8)
- **3** Weakly; dimly (7)
- **4** Inactive (5)
- **5** Symbol or representation (6)
- **6** Engages in combat (6)
- **13** Deceptive (8)
- **14** Copious (7)
- **15** Appeared indistinctly (6)
- **16** Lethargic; sleepy (6)
- **18** Slight prickling sensation (6)
- **19** Departing (5)

PUZZLE 165

1		2		3		4		■	5	6		7
	■		■		■		■	8	■		■	
9					■	10						
	■		■		■		■		■		■	
■	11											
12	■		■		■		■		■	■	■	
13						■	14			15		
	■	■	■		■	16	■		■		■	
17		18										■
	■		■		■		■		■		■	19
20							■	21				
	■		■		■		■		■		■	
22				■	23							

Across

1 Make fun of (8)
5 Group of countries in an alliance (4)
9 Frustrated and annoyed (3,2)
10 However (anag.) (7)
11 Not on purpose; inadvertently (12)
13 Blunt thick needle (6)
14 Rule with authority (6)
17 Restrict within limits (12)
20 Brook (7)
21 Delete (5)
22 Mud (4)
23 Altruistic (8)

Down

1 Repeated jazz phrase (4)
2 Worked out logically (7)
3 Unpredictably (12)
4 Legal practitioner (6)
6 Floor of a building (5)
7 Transporting by hand (8)
8 DIY stands for this (2-2-8)
12 Partially hidden (8)
15 Clasp (7)
16 Insect that transmits sleeping sickness (6)
18 Wanderer (5)
19 Gets married (4)

PUZZLE 166

Across

- **1** Red gem (4)
- **3** Circular representation of data (3,5)
- **9** Hot wind blowing from North Africa (7)
- **10** Bond or connection (5)
- **11** Condemnation (12)
- **13** Ablaze (6)
- **15** Indicator on a computer screen (6)
- **17** Not familiar with or used to (12)
- **20** Tiny crustaceans (5)
- **21** Beat easily (7)
- **22** Fretting (8)
- **23** Close (4)

Down

- **1** Remaining (8)
- **2** Element with atomic number 5 (5)
- **4** Humorously sarcastic (6)
- **5** Building (12)
- **6** Worried and nervous (7)
- **7** Mission (4)
- **8** Thriftily (12)
- **12** Slope (8)
- **14** Taller and thinner (7)
- **16** Jenson ___ : British racing driver (6)
- **18** Period of time consisting of 28 - 31 days (5)
- **19** Slanting; crooked (4)

PUZZLE 167

Across

1 Hasty or reckless (4)
3 Fantastic (8)
9 Mythical being (7)
10 Extremely small (prefix) (5)
11 Long bench (3)
12 Birds lay their eggs in these (5)
13 Burst of light (5)
15 The papal court (5)
17 Completely correct (5)
18 Touch gently (3)
19 Remnant of a dying fire (5)
20 Routers (anag.) (7)
21 Fortified wines (8)
22 Flat-bottomed boat (4)

Down

1 Open-mindedness (13)
2 Tough fibrous tissue (5)
4 Mistakes in printed matter (6)
5 Money paid for work (12)
6 Concentrated on (7)
7 Dealing with different societies (5-8)
8 Maker (12)
14 Woody plant (7)
16 Steal livestock (6)
18 Adhesive substance (5)

PUZZLE 168

Across

4 Wreckage washed ashore (6)
7 Make impossible (8)
8 Annoy (3)
9 Unit of heredity (4)
10 Bracelet (6)
11 Mischief (7)
12 Removes the lid (5)
15 Expel air abruptly (5)
17 Reflects (7)
20 Tentacle (6)
21 Skirt worn by ballerinas (4)
22 Excessively (3)
23 Closely acquainted (8)
24 Element discovered by the Curies (6)

Down

1 Mourn the loss of (6)
2 Crafty; cunning (8)
3 Fourth book of the Bible (7)
4 Clothing made from denim (5)
5 Harsh (6)
6 Sayings (6)
13 Type of employment (4-4)
14 Oscillate (7)
15 Depression from a meteor impact (6)
16 Develop (6)
18 Revolve (6)
19 Assertion (5)

PUZZLE 169

Across

1 Compound found in coffee (8)
5 Spots (4)
9 Puff up; swell (5)
10 Containers (7)
11 Art of planning a dance (12)
14 Boy (3)
15 Protective garment worn in the kitchen (5)
16 Form of public transport (3)
17 Amazement (12)
20 Squeeze into a compact mass (7)
22 Capital of Egypt (5)
23 Relax and do little (4)
24 Concluding section (8)

Down

1 Caribbean country (4)
2 Bubbled (7)
3 Amusing (12)
4 Arrest (3)
6 Crawl (5)
7 Writer of literary works (8)
8 Extremely large (12)
12 Unpleasant giants (5)
13 Skin care product (8)
16 Dressing (7)
18 Ring-shaped object (5)
19 Abode (4)
21 Leap on one foot (3)

PUZZLE 170

Across

1 Foolish (4)
3 Complete loss of electrical power (8)
9 Followed behind (7)
10 Facial protuberances (5)
11 Hostile aggressiveness (12)
13 Text of a play (6)
15 Each (6)
17 Ate too much (12)
20 Ray (5)
21 Bedroom (7)
22 Settlers (anag.) (8)
23 Familiar name for a potato (4)

Down

1 Structured set of information (8)
2 Threshing tool (5)
4 Women (6)
5 Scornful (12)
6 Small bone in the ear (7)
7 Long pointed tooth (4)
8 Crucial (3,9)
12 Offered (8)
14 Income (7)
16 Make possible (6)
18 Assembly (5)
19 Give out (4)

PUZZLE 171

Across

4 Breathless (6)
7 Cocktail (8)
8 Suitable (3)
9 Extent of a surface (4)
10 Leaders (6)
11 Buildings for horses (7)
12 Keep away from (5)
15 Intimidated and weakened (5)
17 Admit (7)
20 Hurries (6)
21 Emperor of Rome 54-68 AD (4)
22 Jewel (3)
23 Midday (8)
24 Hit (6)

Down

1 Orange vegetable (6)
2 Petty quarrel (8)
3 Large jug (7)
4 Fairy (5)
5 Complete failure (6)
6 Marked with small spots (6)
13 Locality (8)
14 Without interruption (3-4)
15 Dogs (6)
16 Hotter (6)
18 Mock (6)
19 Solid piece of something (5)

PUZZLE 172

Across

1 Live (anag.) (4)
3 Recondite (8)
9 Parcel (7)
10 Modify (5)
11 Boldness; courage (5)
12 Throwing a coin in the air (7)
13 Within a space (6)
15 Digit (6)
17 Shut in (7)
18 Pertaining to sound (5)
20 Supply with; furnish (5)
21 Uncomplaining (7)
22 Navigating (8)
23 Refuse to admit (4)

Down

1 Ebullience (13)
2 Bring on oneself (5)
4 Slender (6)
5 Act of sending a message (12)
6 Wandering (7)
7 Unconditionally (13)
8 Person who listens into conversations (12)
14 Isolate (7)
16 Period of instruction (6)
19 Shallow recess (5)

PUZZLE 173

Across

1 e.g. hats and helmets (8)
5 Bucket (4)
9 Fourth month (5)
10 Imposing a tax (7)
11 Clothing such as a vest (12)
13 Had a strong smell (6)
14 Rubs (6)
17 Data about a population (12)
20 Accept to be true (7)
21 Wounded by a wasp (5)
22 Makes a mistake (4)
23 Is composed of (8)

Down

1 Warm up (4)
2 Place in order (7)
3 Birds of prey (6,6)
4 Assert without proof (6)
6 Live by (5)
7 Least heavy (8)
8 Excessive stress (12)
12 Believable (8)
15 Accumulates over time (7)
16 Get by with what is available (4,2)
18 Type of tooth (5)
19 Chickens lay these (4)

PUZZLE 174

Across

1 Mythical sea creatures (8)
5 Photographic material (4)
9 At no time (5)
10 Takes small bites (7)
11 Liberty (7)
12 The beginning of an era (5)
13 Housing (6)
14 Fly an aircraft (6)
17 Deprive of weapons (5)
19 Artistic movement (3,4)
20 Lets in (7)
21 Leaves out (5)
22 Female child (4)
23 Person sent on a special mission (8)

Down

1 Making (13)
2 Critiques (7)
3 Study of the properties of moving air (12)
4 Jeans (6)
6 Snow house (5)
7 Naughtily (13)
8 Perceptions (12)
15 United States (7)
16 Payment for the release of someone (6)
18 Tree of the birch family (5)

PUZZLE 175

Across

1 Simpleton (4)
3 Debatably (8)
9 Completely enveloping (7)
10 Select; choose (5)
11 Picture (12)
13 Swiss city (6)
15 Voice box (6)
17 Making no money (12)
20 Rule (5)
21 Full of jealousy (7)
22 Unstable (8)
23 Cobras (4)

Down

1 e.g. sketches (8)
2 Name applied to something (5)
4 Go back (6)
5 Ugly (12)
6 Scientific study of life (7)
7 Abominable snowman (4)
8 Persistence (12)
12 Overabundances (8)
14 Children's carers (7)
16 Cause to feel upset (6)
18 Printed publications (5)
19 Official language of Pakistan (4)

PUZZLE 176

Across

1 Large barrel (4)
3 Small crustacean (8)
9 Perfect happiness (7)
10 Submerged ridges of rock (5)
11 Theme for a discussion (5)
12 Relating to heat (7)
13 Swollen edible root (6)
15 Dog-like mammals (6)
17 Workshop or studio (7)
18 Door hanger (5)
20 Maladroit (5)
21 River of East Africa (7)
22 Observing (8)
23 Mass of floating ice (4)

Down

1 Dismay and amazement (13)
2 Parts (anag.) (5)
4 Adjusts (6)
5 Short tale told to children (7,5)
6 Ship worker (7)
7 Style of popular music (4,9)
8 Vain (12)
14 Most profound (7)
16 Shamelessly bold (6)
19 Female relation (5)

PUZZLE 177

Across

- **1** Book lover (11)
- **9** Take illegally (5)
- **10** Sound that a cow makes (3)
- **11** Faith in another (5)
- **12** Cleanse by rubbing (5)
- **13** Restore confidence to (8)
- **16** Unscathed (8)
- **18** Domesticates (5)
- **21** Hang with cloth (5)
- **22** Small truck (3)
- **23** Fits of violent anger (5)
- **24** Calculation (11)

Down

- **2** Brutal; cruel (7)
- **3** Boorish (7)
- **4** Of the eye (6)
- **5** Desires (5)
- **6** Arboreal primate (5)
- **7** Another option (11)
- **8** Heavy fire of artillery (11)
- **14** Mobile phone (7)
- **15** Import barrier (7)
- **17** Gold lump (6)
- **19** Juicy fruit (5)
- **20** Sticky sweet liquid (5)

PUZZLE 178

Across

1 Most annoyed (8)
5 Skin mark from a wound (4)
9 Concerning (5)
10 Serving no purpose (7)
11 Someone who sets up their own business (12)
13 Pungent condiment (6)
14 Push over (6)
17 The ? symbol (8,4)
20 Last in a series (7)
21 Horse's cry (5)
22 Spun thread used for knitting (4)
23 Vision (8)

Down

1 First man (4)
2 Adult (5-2)
3 Act of seizing something en route (12)
4 Declines sharply (6)
6 Thin pancake (5)
7 Booked in advance (8)
8 Changes to a situation (12)
12 Obscurely (8)
15 Separating (7)
16 Metrical writing (6)
18 Senior figure in a tribe (5)
19 Converse (4)

PUZZLE 179

Across

1 Eccentricity (11)
9 Spin (5)
10 Legume (3)
11 Mark of repetition (5)
12 Bewildered (5)
13 Calmness under pressure (8)
16 Terrible (8)
18 Unabridged (5)
21 Performing a deed (5)
22 Legal ruling (3)
23 Thing that imparts motion (5)
24 Perplexing situation (11)

Down

2 Version of a book (7)
3 Relaxed (7)
4 Phrases that are not taken literally (6)
5 Angered; irritated (5)
6 Precious gem (5)
7 Boldly (11)
8 Weak form of illumination (11)
14 Tympanic membrane (7)
15 e.g. from Ethiopia (7)
17 Simple; unrefined (6)
19 Crouch down in fear (5)
20 Shy (5)

PUZZLE 180

1		2		3		4		■	5	6		7
	■		■		■		■	8	■		■	
9					■	10						
	■		■		■	■	■		■		■	
■	11					12						
13	■		■		■		■		■	■	■	
14			■	15					■	16		
	■	■	■		■		■		■		■	
17		18										■
	■		■		■	■	■		■		■	19
20						21	■	22				
	■		■		■		■		■		■	
23				■	24							

Across

1 Delays it (anag.) (8)
5 Temporary living quarters (4)
9 Legal process (5)
10 Distress (7)
11 Thick-skinned herbivorous animal (12)
14 Pub (3)
15 Less moist (5)
16 Fish appendage (3)
17 Very upsetting (5-7)
20 Ancient jar (7)
22 A satellite of Uranus (5)
23 Pay close attention to (4)
24 Substance causing a reaction (8)

Down

1 Takes an exam (4)
2 Omission of a sound when speaking (7)
3 State of being in disrepair (12)
4 Auction item (3)
6 Collection of songs (5)
7 Agreeable (8)
8 Person studying after a first degree (12)
12 Balance (5)
13 Confused mixture (8)
16 Sport using swords (7)
18 Plentiful (5)
19 Large family (4)
21 Tool for making holes in leather (3)

PUZZLE 181

Across

1 A cause of great trouble (11)
9 Armature of an electric motor (5)
10 Container for a drink (3)
11 Given to disclosing secrets (5)
12 Dance club (5)
13 Commonplace (8)
16 Water-resistant jacket (8)
18 Golf course sections (5)
21 Diacritical mark (5)
22 Ram (anag.) (3)
23 Allow entry to (5)
24 Gathering information (4-7)

Down

2 Sends back into custody (7)
3 Hiding underground (7)
4 Alphabetical character (6)
5 Weary (5)
6 Killer whales (5)
7 General guideline (4,2,5)
8 Engagement (11)
14 Made a garment by intertwining threads (7)
15 Sad and abandoned (7)
17 Graduates of an academic institution (6)
19 Insect grub (5)
20 Viewpoint or angle (5)

PUZZLE 182

Across

1 Cunning (4)
3 Coaches (8)
9 Not tense (7)
10 Trembling poplar (5)
11 Beginning (12)
14 Touch gently (3)
16 Ticks over (5)
17 Sense of self-esteem (3)
18 Best starting placement in a motor race (4,8)
21 Card game (5)
22 One thousand million (7)
23 Shows (8)
24 Mischievous sprites (4)

Down

1 Savage fierceness (8)
2 Woody tissue (5)
4 Fishing pole (3)
5 Not allowable (12)
6 Cost (7)
7 Male children (4)
8 Based on untested ideas (12)
12 Stringed instrument (5)
13 These precede afternoons (8)
15 Financial gains (7)
19 Form of expression (5)
20 Still to be paid (4)
22 Broad inlet of the sea (3)

PUZZLE 183

Across

1 Applications (4)
3 Disloyal people (8)
9 Relating to what you eat (7)
10 Outdo (5)
11 Assesses performance (5)
12 Prior (7)
13 Huge desert in North Africa (6)
15 Savage (6)
17 Hindered (7)
18 Speed music is played at (5)
20 Loft (5)
21 Evident (7)
22 Encrypting (8)
23 Resist; refuse to obey (4)

Down

1 Value too lowly (13)
2 Upright (5)
4 Had corresponding sounds (6)
5 Explanatory (12)
6 Type of optician (7)
7 In a manner that exceeds what is necessary (13)
8 Made in bulk (4-8)
14 Pertaining to the liver (7)
16 Border (6)
19 Large deer (5)

PUZZLE 184

Across

1 Fearless and brave (8)
5 Engrave with acid (4)
9 Join together; merge (5)
10 Summit (7)
11 Indicator (7)
12 Person who eats in a restaurant (5)
13 District (6)
14 Swordsman (6)
17 Enlighten; educate (5)
19 Anapest (anag.) (7)
20 Spicy Spanish sausage (7)
21 Conjuring trick (5)
22 Stage of twilight (4)
23 Act of retaliation (8)

Down

1 Wet behind the ears (13)
2 Working hard (7)
3 Decomposition by a current (12)
4 Exist permanently in (6)
6 Colossus (5)
7 Excessively negative about (13)
8 Heavy long-handled tool (12)
15 Modifies (7)
16 Argue against (6)
18 Images of deities (5)

PUZZLE 185

Across

1 Dominion (4)
3 Teacher (8)
9 Stingy (7)
10 Conventions (5)
11 Relating to farming (12)
14 Half of four (3)
16 Should (5)
17 Be in debt (3)
18 Fully extended (12)
21 Pass a rope through (5)
22 Outline; silhouette (7)
23 Creative (8)
24 Ewers (4)

Down

1 Defensive walls (8)
2 Focused light beam (5)
4 Not wet (3)
5 Act of discussing something; deliberation (12)
6 Cyclone (7)
7 Optimistic (4)
8 Courtesy (12)
12 Beer (5)
13 Careless (8)
15 Affluent (7)
19 Type of poem (5)
20 Killer whale (4)
22 21st Greek letter (3)

PUZZLE 186

Across

1 Put in order (4)
3 Places of refuge (8)
9 Mechanical keyboard (7)
10 Strength (5)
11 Very cold (3)
12 Garbage or drivel (5)
13 Deciduous coniferous tree (5)
15 Cry out loudly (5)
17 Complains continually (5)
18 Cooking utensil (3)
19 Half of six (5)
20 Hair-cleansing product (7)
21 Topsides (anag.) (8)
22 Mountain system in Europe (4)

Down

1 Refined (13)
2 Fully prepared (5)
4 Public speaker (6)
5 Conjectural (12)
6 Despicable person (7)
7 Clandestine (13)
8 Vagrancy (12)
14 Deliver by parachute (3-4)
16 Compensate for (6)
18 Proceeding from the pope (5)

PUZZLE 187

Across

1 Person with strong patriotic feelings (11)
9 Place of refuge (5)
10 Hairpiece (3)
11 Punctuation mark (5)
12 Mountain cry (5)
13 Rain tree (anag.) (8)
16 Value greatly (8)
18 Amusing people (5)
21 Destiny; fate (5)
22 Carry a heavy object (3)
23 Crumble (5)
24 Distribute again (11)

Down

2 Horizontal angle of a compass bearing (7)
3 Live in (7)
4 Beginner (6)
5 Tall and thin (5)
6 Stitched (5)
7 Wrongly (11)
8 Form into a cluster (11)
14 Most poorly lit (7)
15 Tortilla rolled around a filling (7)
17 Style of art or architecture (6)
19 Scoundrel (5)
20 Engross oneself in (5)

PUZZLE 188

Across

1 Catholic leader (4)
3 Person with a degree (8)
9 Pieces of bacon (7)
10 Join together (5)
11 Consume food (3)
12 Original (5)
13 Travels by bicycle (5)
15 Lighter (5)
17 Ancient measure of length (5)
18 Body's vital life force (3)
19 Foreign language (informal) (5)
20 Vending (7)
21 Musical composition (8)
22 Extremely (4)

Down

1 Upright; vertical (13)
2 Suggest (5)
4 Took it easy (6)
5 Clearly evident (12)
6 Reached a destination (7)
7 Eternally (13)
8 Detailed reports (12)
14 European country (7)
16 Hired out (6)
18 Felony (5)

PUZZLE 189

Across

1 Dour help (anag.) (8)
5 Song for a solo voice (4)
9 Religious acts (5)
10 Extinguish a candle (4,3)
11 Climbing plant (7)
12 Misgiving (5)
13 Records on tape (6)
14 Small gadget (6)
17 Indian monetary unit (5)
19 Of great size (7)
20 Noisy confusion (7)
21 Waggish (5)
22 Fencing sword (4)
23 Shop selling medicinal drugs (8)

Down

1 Irretrievable (13)
2 Impetuous person (7)
3 Repository for misplaced items (4,8)
4 Glowing remains of a fire (6)
6 Dry red wine (5)
7 In a reflex manner (13)
8 Spanish adventurer (12)
15 Venetian boat (7)
16 Complex carbohydrate (6)
18 Long cloud of smoke (5)

PUZZLE 190

Across

1 Incidental activity (6)
7 Outlines in detail (8)
8 Argument against something (3)
9 Good luck charm (6)
10 Shaft on which a wheel rotates (4)
11 Put in position (5)
13 Series of boat races (7)
15 Dispensers (7)
17 Business proposal; playing field (5)
21 Release (4)
22 A size of book page (6)
23 Fruit preserve (3)
24 e.g. from Tokyo (8)
25 Poem of fourteen lines (6)

Down

1 Help or support (6)
2 Country in Central America (6)
3 Screams (5)
4 Emit spitting sounds (7)
5 Squid dish (8)
6 Bangle worn at the top of the foot (6)
12 Raised road (8)
14 Game played on a lawn (7)
16 Move apart; open out (6)
18 Inhabitant of Troy (6)
19 Recluse (6)
20 Dislikes intensely (5)

PUZZLE 191

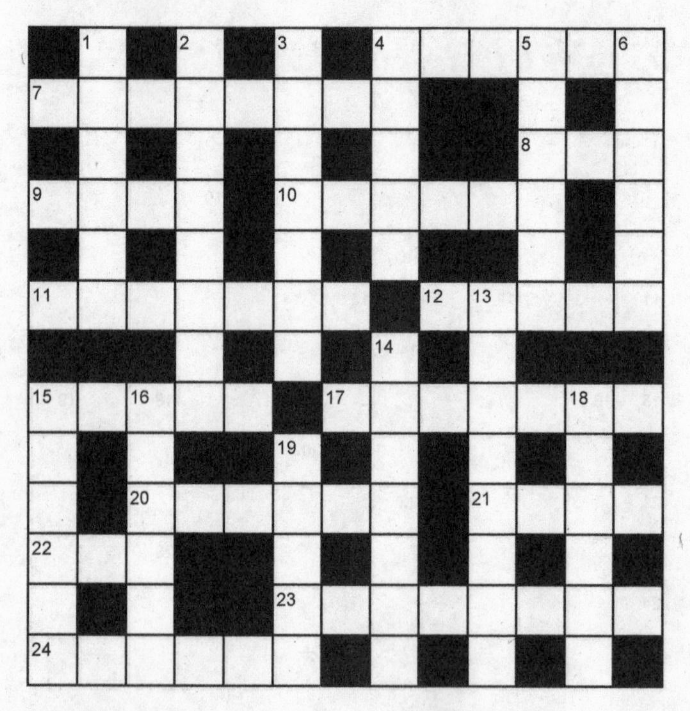

Across

4 Involuntary spasm (6)
7 Aromatic plant used in cooking (8)
8 Playing card (3)
9 Sparkling wine (4)
10 Move with a bounding motion (6)
11 Scorn (7)
12 Coiled curve (5)
15 Intoxicating (5)
17 Part of a golf course (7)
20 Raised (6)
21 Strong and healthy (4)
22 Gone by (of time) (3)
23 Familiar description for a person (8)
24 Finishing (6)

Down

1 Inborn (6)
2 Renovated (8)
3 Having no purpose at all (7)
4 Greets with enthusiasm (5)
5 Place of worship (6)
6 Title placed before a name (6)
13 Grounding (of electricity) (8)
14 Small field (7)
15 Showing compassion (6)
16 Overseas (6)
18 Assurance; composure (6)
19 Mistaken (5)

PUZZLE 192

Across

1 Short hollow thud (4)
3 Small turtle (8)
9 Friendly understanding (7)
10 Schemes (5)
11 Shyness (12)
14 Twitch (3)
16 Fit with glass (5)
17 Come together (3)
18 Recovering from illness (of a person) (12)
21 Promotional wording (5)
22 Eighth sign of the zodiac (7)
23 Emaciated (8)
24 Woes (4)

Down

1 Foretells (8)
2 Group of eight (5)
4 Make a living with difficulty (3)
5 Act of reclamation (12)
6 Increase the duration of (7)
7 Facial feature (4)
8 Not excusable (12)
12 Electronic communication (5)
13 Military units (8)
15 Sense of resolution (7)
19 Kick out (5)
20 Recedes (4)
22 Belgian town (3)

PUZZLE 193

Across

1 Dealing with (8)
5 Fish (4)
8 Naves (anag.) (5)
9 Totally (7)
10 Statement of commemoration (7)
12 Rocket stage giving initial acceleration (7)
14 Tell a story (7)
16 Grotesque monster (7)
18 Sets out on a journey (7)
19 Drain away from soil (of a chemical) (5)
20 Type of starch (4)
21 Self-operating machines (8)

Down

1 Bee colony (4)
2 Papal representative (6)
3 Lack of energy (9)
4 Not masculine or feminine (6)
6 Raise up (6)
7 Not in a specific location (8)
11 Very confused situation (9)
12 Burns slightly or chars (8)
13 Safety device in a car (6)
14 Capital of the Bahamas (6)
15 Domesticated llama (6)
17 Ostrichlike bird (4)

PUZZLE 194

Across

1 Sport popular in America (8)
5 Quartz-like gem (4)
9 Unbuttoned (5)
10 Warding (anag.) (7)
11 Quiver (7)
12 Send money (5)
13 Remains preserved in rock (6)
14 Opposite of an acid (6)
17 Fat-like compound (5)
19 Insulating material (7)
20 Large area of land (7)
21 Possessor (5)
22 Observed (4)
23 Leaning at an angle (8)

Down

1 Copious abundance (13)
2 Makes unhappy (7)
3 Process of enlarging one's muscles (12)
4 Book of accounts (6)
6 Solid geometric figure (5)
7 Prone to steal (5-8)
8 Blasphemous (12)
15 Arranged neatly (7)
16 Ratio of reflected to incident light (6)
18 Immature insects (5)

PUZZLE 195

Across

4 Estimated (6)
7 Raider (8)
8 Wetland (3)
9 Bird of prey (4)
10 What a spider spins (6)
11 e.g. a bishop (7)
12 Person invited to one's house (5)
15 Striped insects (5)
17 Afternoon performance (7)
20 16 of these in a pound (6)
21 An individual thing (4)
22 Propel a boat (3)
23 Fit together easily (8)
24 Songlike cries (6)

Down

1 Type of market (6)
2 Reverse somersault (8)
3 Instruct (7)
4 Insect larvae (5)
5 Speak rapidly (6)
6 Type of canoe (6)
13 Omnipresence (8)
14 Huge (7)
15 Sailing barge (6)
16 Decreased one's speed (6)
18 Evoke (6)
19 Rushes along; skims (5)

PUZZLE 196

Across

1 Seed case (4)
3 Block (8)
9 Study of rocks (7)
10 Stares at in a lecherous way (5)
11 Working for oneself (4-8)
14 Tree (3)
16 Joining together with cord (5)
17 Turn upside down (3)
18 Very exciting (12)
21 Pastoral poem (5)
22 Film directed by Stephen Gaghan (7)
23 Irritating (8)
24 Legendary story (4)

Down

1 International waters (4,4)
2 Frown (5)
4 Lad (3)
5 Street (12)
6 Least attractive (7)
7 Check; exam (4)
8 Nationally (12)
12 Earlier (5)
13 Engraved inscription (8)
15 Marked by prosperity (of a past time) (7)
19 European country (5)
20 Document allowing entry to a country (4)
22 Male offspring (3)

PUZZLE 197

Across

1 Being with organic and cybernetic parts (6)
7 Conversation between two people (3-2-3)
8 Fix the result in advance (3)
9 Legitimate (6)
10 Woody plant (4)
11 Enumerates (5)
13 Bad-tempered (7)
15 Receptacle for cigarette residue (7)
17 Got to one's feet (5)
21 Silent (4)
22 System of doing things (6)
23 Decay (3)
24 Notes of a chord played in rapid succession (8)
25 Small carnivorous mammal (6)

Down

1 Claret (anag.) (6)
2 Brass instruments (6)
3 Silly (5)
4 Basements (7)
5 Teach (8)
6 Entangle (6)
12 Tied up (8)
14 Artificial barrier in a watercourse (7)
16 Eject liquid in a jet (6)
18 Musical dramas (6)
19 Metrical foot (6)
20 Softly radiant (5)

PUZZLE 198

Across

1 Animal enclosure (4)
3 Musical instrument (8)
9 Amino acid (7)
10 Overly sentimental (5)
11 Disturbance; act of meddling (12)
14 Periodic publication (abbrev.) (3)
16 Peak (5)
17 Snow runner (3)
18 Insistently (12)
21 Allowed by official rules (5)
22 Exuberantly joyful (7)
23 Strip of land by a highway (8)
24 Sight organs (4)

Down

1 Personal magnetism (8)
2 Allot; allocate money (5)
4 First woman (3)
5 Wearing glasses (12)
6 Characteristics (7)
7 24-hour periods (4)
8 Type of cloud (12)
12 Expel (5)
13 Two-wheeled vehicles (8)
15 State of the USA (7)
19 Towering (5)
20 Smudge (4)
22 Superhuman being (3)

PUZZLE 199

Across

1 Gangs (4)
3 Capital of Australia (8)
9 Odd (7)
10 Slopes (5)
11 Smooth and easy progress (5,7)
13 Denial (anag.) (6)
15 Raise for discussion (6)
17 Happiness (12)
20 Glazed earthenware (5)
21 Disentangle (7)
22 Finely chopped (8)
23 Saw; observed (4)

Down

1 Squander money (8)
2 Former name of Myanmar (5)
4 Stadiums (6)
5 Electronic security device (7,5)
6 European country (7)
7 Too; in addition (4)
8 Indifferent to (12)
12 Made a high-pitched sound (8)
14 Item used by asthma sufferers (7)
16 Exude (6)
18 Representative; messenger (5)
19 Sums together (4)

PUZZLE 200

Across

1 Word that qualifies another (6)
7 Ill feeling (8)
8 A man's dinner jacket (abbrev.) (3)
9 Money received (6)
10 Rank (4)
11 Opposite of lows (5)
13 Jumpers (7)
15 Young pilchard (7)
17 Core group; basic unit (5)
21 Drive away (4)
22 Change gradually (6)
23 For each (3)
24 Starlike symbol (8)
25 Parts of church towers (6)

Down

1 Join or fasten (6)
2 Annoying (6)
3 Relay device (5)
4 Cleaned its feathers (of a bird) (7)
5 Food of the gods (8)
6 Very difficult or complex (6)
12 Lightest chemical element (8)
14 Segmented worm (7)
16 Struck by overwhelming shock (6)
18 More profound (6)
19 Background actors (6)
20 Residents of an abbey (5)

SOLUTIONS

1

D	I	M	I	N	I	S	H		P	A	I	R
E		U		A		I				N		E
B	E	S	E	T		T	E	L	A	V	I	V
T		E		U		U				I		E
		U		R		P	E	D	D	L	E	R
M	A	M	M	A	L	S		I		S		E
A				L				S				N
N		S		L		S	U	P	P	O	R	T
D	E	C	R	Y	P	T		E		U		
A		R				A		R		T		F
T	E	E	M	I	N	G		S	E	W	E	R
E		A				E		A		I		A
S	U	M	S		I	D	O	L	A	T	R	Y

2

M	U	R	K		S	C	R	I	B	B	L	E
O		E		B		I		N		R		R
T	E	N	S	I	O	N		T	H	O	R	N
H		E		B		D		I		W		E
B	E	W	I	L	D	E	R	M	E	N	T	
A				I		R		I		I		S
L	I	Q	U	O	R		O	D	D	E	S	T
L		U		G		O		A				R
	D	I	S	R	E	P	U	T	A	B	L	E
C		E		A		T		I		E		S
L	E	T	U	P		I	G	N	O	R	E	S
E		E		H		M		G		Y		E
F	U	N	N	Y	M	A	N		P	L	O	D

3

U	N	F	A	I	R	L	Y		S	H	O	T
N		L		M		O		M		I		R
A	X	I	O	M		W	R	E	S	T	L	E
C		P		E		E		T		C		A
C	O	P	R	A		S		A		H	I	S
O		E		S	E	T	U	P				U
U		D		U				H		P		R
N				R	E	P	L	Y		L		E
T	E	A		A		R		S	T	A	R	T
A		L		B		O		I		I		R
B	O	O	K	L	E	T		C	O	N	G	O
L		N		E		E		A		L		V
E	R	G	O		E	M	P	L	O	Y	E	E

4

	S	P	R	I	N	G	C	L	E	A	N	
R		R		N		A		O		N		I
E		E		T	O	N	I	C		D	I	M
S	O	L	V	E		N		A		E		P
E		U		N		E		L	O	S	E	R
M	E	D	I	T	A	T	E					O
B		E		S				L		L		V
L					I	N	S	E	C	U	R	E
A	L	L	E	Y		E		A		M		M
N		A		E		A		F	A	B	L	E
C	A	T		M	O	R	A	L		A		N
E		E		E		E		E		G		T
	E	X	O	N	E	R	A	T	I	O	N	

5

A	I	R	E	D	A	L	E		O	D	D	S
U		E		E		O		P		E		E
T	O	T	A	L		S	P	E	C	I	A	L
O		O		I		E		R		S		F
B	L	U	B	B	E	R		S	A	M	B	A
I		C		E		S		P				W
O	T	H	E	R	S		S	I	E	R	R	A
G				A		A		R		A		R
R	O	B	O	T		T	R	A	M	P	L	E
A		L		E		O		T		T		N
P	R	E	P	L	A	N		I	N	U	R	E
H		A		Y		A		O		R		S
Y	O	K	E		S	L	A	N	D	E	R	S

6

R	O	A	M		O	B	L	I	G	I	N	G
E		D		T		U		N		M		U
C	L	E	A	R	L	Y		D	O	P	E	Y
R		P		A				I		R		S
E	X	T	I	N	G	U	I	S	H	E	R	
A				S		L		C		S		P
T	O	W		P	E	T	E	R		S	I	R
E		A		A		R		E				E
	O	V	E	R	C	A	U	T	I	O	U	S
W		E		E				I		N		S
H	E	R	O	N		F	L	O	T	S	A	M
E		E		C		U		N		E		E
T	A	R	R	Y	I	N	G		S	T	U	N

7

M	E	R	R	I	E	S	T		G	R	U	B
A		E		N		A		S		I		A
P	A	C	E	D		C	H	E	R	V	I	L
S		O		E				L		A		L
	P	U	R	P	O	S	E	F	U	L	L	Y
T		N		E		C		L				H
H	I	T		N	O	O	S	E		G	O	O
U				D		U		S		E		O
M	I	S	R	E	P	R	E	S	E	N	T	
B		A		N				N		E		D
S	O	L	I	C	I	T		E	E	R	I	E
U		O		E		A		S		A		A
P	O	N	G		W	R	E	S	T	L	E	R

8

A	W	A	Y		C	A	U	C	U	S	E	S
C		S		A		R		U		N		A
R	O	S	T	R	U	M		R	O	O	M	Y
O		E		T				M		R		S
S	I	T	T	I	N	G	D	U	C	K	S	
T				S		R		D		E		O
I	L	L		T	W	A	N	G		L	O	B
C		E		I		I		E				S
	D	I	S	C	O	N	S	O	L	A	T	E
C		S		A				N		C		S
E	Q	U	A	L		U	N	L	O	C	K	S
D		R		L		S		Y		R		E
E	V	E	R	Y	D	A	Y		N	A	G	S

9

A	N	T	I	D	O	T	E		E	T	N	A
U		R		E		A		S		H		S
T	R	A	W	L		W	I	T	L	E	S	S
H		F		I		D		R		F		E
O	F	F	I	C	E	R		A	C	T	O	R
R		I		A		Y		I				T
I	N	C	I	T	E		A	G	O	U	T	I
T				E		D		H		P		V
A	M	A	S	S		A	R	T	I	S	T	E
R		N		S		H		E		U		N
I	N	K	W	E	L	L		N	U	R	S	E
A		L		N		I		E		G		S
N	O	E	S		B	A	L	D	N	E	S	S

10

O	U	S	T		A	V	O	C	A	D	O	S
R		T		A		I		O		I		I
T	H	E	O	R	E	M		U	P	S	E	T
H		E		I				N		P		E
O	B	L	I	T	E	R	A	T	I	O	N	
D				H		A		R		S		P
O	R	C		M	U	R	K	Y		E	L	L
X		H		E		E		W				A
	V	I	C	T	O	R	I	O	U	S	L	Y
A		G		I				M		P		B
T	U	N	I	C		S	C	A	P	U	L	A
O		O		A		A		N		M		C
M	O	N	O	L	I	T	H		B	E	A	K

11

B	O	U	D	O	I	R	S		G	L	U	E
I		T		L		E		D		A		M
D	R	I	E	D		C	H	E	C	K	U	P
S		L		F		I		M		E		T
	D	I	S	A	S	T	R	O	U	S	L	Y
T		T		S		E		N				I
R	H	Y	T	H	M		A	S	T	E	R	N
O				I		S		T		Q		G
P	R	E	P	O	S	T	E	R	O	U	S	
I		X		N		A		A		A		N
C	L	E	M	E	N	T		T	I	T	H	E
A		R		D		U		O		O		A
L	U	T	E		T	E	A	R	D	R	O	P

12

M	A	S	K		B	A	G	U	E	T	T	E
A		P		I		B		N		R		A
G	R	O	U	N	D	S		E	X	I	T	S
I		O		C		O		X		R		Y
C	A	R	T	O	G	R	A	P	H	E	R	
I				N		B		E		M		R
A	R	T	I	S	T		A	C	C	E	D	E
N		R		I		S		T				C
	C	O	N	S	E	Q	U	E	N	T	L	Y
T		D		T		U		D		I		C
H	E	D	G	E		I	L	L	E	G	A	L
U		E		N		N		Y		E		E
S	A	N	C	T	I	T	Y		O	R	B	S

13

■	T	R	I	C	E	R	A	T	O	P	S	■
C	■	E	■	Y	■	E	■	O	■	E	■	R
O	■	S	■	C	H	A	R	D	■	A	P	E
N	A	T	A	L	■	S	■	A	■	C	■	C
S	■	F	■	O	■	O	■	Y	A	H	O	O
T	H	U	M	P	I	N	G	■	■	■	■	M
R	■	L	■	S	■	■	■	P	■	H	■	M
I	■	■	■	■	A	C	T	I	V	A	T	E
C	H	A	F	F	■	A	■	T	■	R	■	N
T	■	F	■	E	■	T	■	F	A	D	E	D
O	F	F	■	M	A	N	I	A	■	H	■	E
R	■	I	■	U	■	A	■	L	■	A	■	D
■	E	X	T	R	A	P	O	L	A	T	E	■

14

I	N	S	T	A	N	C	E	■	A	P	E	S
N	■	Y	■	R	■	L	■	H	■	L	■	H
V	I	S	O	R	■	A	V	O	C	A	D	O
E	■	T	■	A	■	I	■	R	■	Z	■	O
S	T	E	R	N	U	M	■	R	O	A	S	T
T	■	M	■	G	■	S	■	O	■	■	■	I
I	N	S	T	E	P	■	P	R	O	T	O	N
G	■	■	■	M	■	M	■	S	■	E	■	G
A	D	A	G	E	■	I	N	T	O	N	E	S
T	■	X	■	N	■	S	■	R	■	A	■	T
I	D	I	O	T	I	C	■	U	M	B	R	A
O	■	N	■	S	■	U	■	C	■	L	■	R
N	I	G	H	■	W	E	A	K	N	E	S	S

15

■	C	L	E	A	R	H	E	A	D	E	D	■
M	■	A	■	T	■	U	■	B	■	N	■	S
I	V	Y	■	O	A	S	I	S	■	L	■	U
C	■	E	■	L	■	T	■	C	L	A	S	P
R	U	R	A	L	■	L	■	O	■	R	■	E
O	■	■	■	■	T	E	E	N	A	G	E	R
S	■	U	■	D	■	■	■	D	■	E	■	F
C	O	N	T	E	M	P	T	■	■	■	■	I
O	■	U	■	B	■	E	■	D	O	R	I	C
P	O	S	E	R	■	R	■	O	■	E	■	I
E	■	U	■	I	C	I	L	Y	■	V	I	A
S	■	A	■	E	■	S	■	E	■	U	■	L
■	C	L	I	F	F	H	A	N	G	E	R	■

16

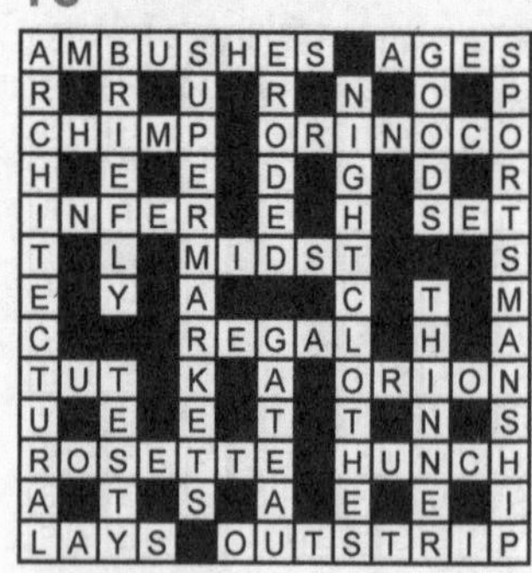

A	M	B	U	S	H	E	S	■	A	G	E	S
R	■	R	■	U	■	R	■	N	■	O	■	P
C	H	I	M	P	■	O	R	I	N	O	C	O
H	■	E	■	E	■	D	■	G	■	D	■	R
I	N	F	E	R	■	E	■	H	■	S	E	T
T	■	L	■	M	I	D	S	T	■	■	■	S
E	■	Y	■	A	■	■	■	C	■	T	■	M
C	■	■	■	R	E	G	A	L	■	H	■	A
T	U	T	■	K	■	A	■	O	R	I	O	N
U	■	E	■	E	■	T	■	T	■	N	■	S
R	O	S	E	T	T	E	■	H	U	N	C	H
A	■	T	■	S	■	A	■	E	■	E	■	I
L	A	Y	S	■	O	U	T	S	T	R	I	P

17

R	E	D	E	P	L	O	Y	■	A	B	L	E
E	■	O	■	R	■	U	■	D	■	R	■	F
M	O	U	S	E	■	S	P	I	N	O	F	F
O	■	B	■	D	■	T	■	N	■	A	■	E
R	E	L	I	E	V	E	■	N	A	D	I	R
S	■	E	■	C	■	D	■	E	■	■	■	V
E	D	D	I	E	S	■	G	R	O	O	V	E
L	■	■	■	S	■	A	■	J	■	U	■	S
E	T	H	O	S	■	D	R	A	S	T	I	C
S	■	U	■	O	■	M	■	C	■	D	■	E
S	A	M	U	R	A	I	■	K	N	O	W	N
L	■	A	■	S	■	R	■	E	■	N	■	C
Y	A	N	K	■	A	E	S	T	H	E	T	E

18

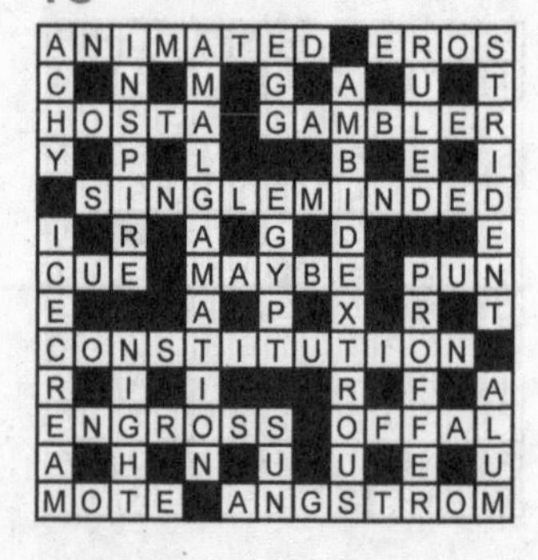

A	N	I	M	A	T	E	D	■	E	R	O	S
C	■	N	■	M	■	G	■	A	■	U	■	T
H	O	S	T	A	■	G	A	M	B	L	E	R
Y	■	P	■	L	■	■	■	B	■	E	■	I
■	S	I	N	G	L	E	M	I	N	D	E	D
I	■	R	■	A	■	G	■	D	■	■	■	E
C	U	E	■	M	A	Y	B	E	■	P	U	N
E	■	■	■	A	■	P	■	X	■	R	■	T
C	O	N	S	T	I	T	U	T	I	O	N	■
R	■	I	■	I	■	■	■	R	■	F	■	A
E	N	G	R	O	S	S	■	O	F	F	A	L
A	■	H	■	N	■	U	■	U	■	E	■	U
M	O	T	E	■	A	N	G	S	T	R	O	M

19

E	S	C	A	P	I	S	T		S	P	I	N
R		H		R		P		I		O		O
A	M	U	S	E		L	A	N	O	L	I	N
S		F		R		I		H		K		S
	A	F	F	E	C	T	I	O	N	A	T	E
I		E		Q		S		S				N
M	A	D	E	U	P		S	P	E	A	K	S
M				I		P		I		N		E
U	N	S	U	S	P	E	C	T	I	N	G	
N		E		I		R		A		E		A
I	M	P	E	T	U	S		B	O	X	E	R
T		A		E		O		L		E		K
Y	A	L	E		I	N	V	E	R	S	E	S

20

C	L	E	N	C	H	E	S		S	W	I	G
O		N		O		B		I		E		U
G	I	V	E	N		B	O	N	F	I	R	E
S		E		V				C		G		S
	P	L	A	I	N	C	L	O	T	H	E	S
K		O		N		E		M				I
I	M	P		C	L	A	M	P		M	A	N
N				I		S		A		U		G
D	I	S	I	N	T	E	G	R	A	T	E	
L		I		G				A		A		P
I	N	D	U	L	G	E		B	I	B	L	E
N		E		Y		R		L		L		L
G	A	S	P		C	A	S	E	M	E	N	T

21

D	I	S	T	I	N	C	T		D	O	U	R
O		U		N		A		P		S		I
M	I	G	H	T		V	O	I	C	I	N	G
E		G		E		E		T		E		H
S	M	E	L	L		R		T		R	A	T
T		S		L	A	N	C	E				E
I		T		I				R		E		O
C				G	E	T	U	P		X		U
A	S	P		E		I		A	C	I	D	S
T		E		N		S		T		G		N
I	N	D	U	C	E	S		T	H	E	M	E
O		A		E		U		E		N		S
N	U	L	L		D	E	T	R	I	T	U	S

22

B	U	M	P		F	O	R	S	O	O	T	H
I		O		T		N		H		P		I
O	U	T	G	R	O	W		O	W	I	N	G
D		E		A		A		R		N		H
E	A	T	E	N		R	E	T	S	I	N	A
G				S		D		C		O		N
R	E	L	I	C	S		P	I	N	N	E	D
A		O		E		C		R				M
D	I	U	R	N	A	L		C	O	R	G	I
A		D		D		O		U		O		G
B	R	E	V	E		T	R	I	U	M	P	H
L		S		N		H		T		A		T
E	N	T	I	T	L	E	D		O	N	L	Y

23

R	E	S	E	M	B	L	E		S	A	I	D
E		A		U		O		A		V		I
V	I	N	Y	L		U	N	D	R	E	S	S
E		D		T		N		V		R		A
R	I	P	P	I	N	G		A	E	S	O	P
B		I		L		E		N				P
E	N	T	R	A	P		S	T	A	B	L	E
R				T		F		A		O		A
A	I	S	L	E		R	E	G	U	L	A	R
T		T		R		E		E		S		A
I	S	O	B	A	R	S		O	F	T	E	N
O		I		L		C		U		E		C
N	I	C	E		C	O	N	S	T	R	U	E

24

C	U	F	F		M	A	R	M	O	S	E	T
O		L		R		S		O		C		E
N	E	A	T	E	N	S		T	H	E	R	M
S		I		F		I		I		N		P
E	R	R	O	R		G	A	V	O	T	T	E
Q				E		N		A		E		R
U	N	R	E	S	T		S	T	A	D	I	A
E		E		H		I		I				M
N	I	P	P	I	N	G		O	P	I	N	E
T		L		N		U		N		M		N
I	C	I	N	G		A	D	A	M	A	N	T
A		C		L		N		L		G		A
L	E	A	P	Y	E	A	R		D	O	L	L

25

	M		C		S		S	E	N	S	O	R
D	O	O	R	S	T	O	P			I		O
	D		E		U		L			G	A	B
P	U	M	A		T	H	A	T	C	H		B
	L		T		T		T			E		E
S	E	D	U	C	E	S		J	A	D	E	D
			R		R		T		L			
P	I	P	E	D		B	U	C	K	L	E	S
L		R			M		R		A		N	
A		A	T	T	A	I	N		L	A	T	H
T	O	N			D		I		I		A	
E		K			A	P	P	E	N	D	I	X
S	Y	S	T	E	M		S		E		L	

26

	A	M	E	L	I	O	R	A	T	E	S	
C		A		A		P		C		A		E
O		S		W	I	P	E	R		G	U	M
R	E	T	R	Y		U		E		L		B
R		I		E		G		S	T	E	E	R
O	F	F	E	R	I	N	G					O
B		F		S				C		T		I
O					R	E	Q	U	I	R	E	D
R	I	S	E	S		V		T		I		E
A		I		A		O		D	E	B	A	R
T	I	N		T	O	K	Y	O		U		E
E		G		Y		E		W		T		R
	R	E	P	R	E	S	E	N	T	E	D	

27

M	U	S	I	C	I	A	N		W	A	R	M
O		E		A		S				B		A
S	W	E	A	R		S	I	M	P	L	E	R
T		K		T		A				O		K
		E		R		I	M	P	I	O	U	S
M	A	R	T	I	A	L		O		M		M
Y				D				R				A
T		F		G		S	E	C	T	I	O	N
H	A	R	V	E	S	T		E		D		
I		A				E		L		I		B
C	A	N	T	E	E	N		A	R	O	S	E
A		C				C		I		C		A
L	I	E	N		T	H	A	N	K	Y	O	U

28

S	U	R	V	I	V	O	R		I	C	E	S
O		E		N		B		C		A		P
L	I	C	I	T		S	C	H	E	R	Z	O
E		O		E		E		I		A		N
	C	I	R	R	O	S	T	R	A	T	U	S
P		L		M		S		O				O
E	N	S	U	E	S		S	P	I	D	E	R
R				D		B		R		E		S
S	I	G	N	I	F	I	C	A	N	C	E	
I		A		A		R		C		L		B
S	P	U	R	R	E	D		T	E	A	R	Y
T		Z		Y		I		O		R		T
S	E	E	R		R	E	T	R	I	E	V	E

29

T	Y	P	I	S	T		S		D		R	
O		I			H	A	M	M	E	R	E	D
W	A	R			A		U		M		P	
E		A	V	O	W	E	D		O	B	E	Y
L		T			S		G		L		A	
S	E	E	M	S		D	E	V	I	A	T	E
			O		O		S		S			
A	B	S	O	R	B	S		T	H	R	O	W
	R		R		S		B			U		I
K	I	W	I		C	H	E	R	U	B		N
	D		N		U		S			R	I	D
K	A	N	G	A	R	O	O			I		O
	L		S		E		M	O	S	C	O	W

30

P	E	N	K	N	I	F	E		S	W	A	M
A		U		O		E		B		A		E
R	I	P	E	N		D	R	O	U	G	H	T
A		T		F		O		T		E		A
P	H	I	A	L		R		T		R	A	M
H		A		A	V	A	I	L				O
E		L		M				E		M		R
R				M	A	C	R	O		A		P
N	U	T		A		A		P	O	R	C	H
A		H		B		N		E		T		O
L	O	Y	A	L	T	Y		N	A	I	L	S
I		M		E		O		E		A		I
A	M	E	N		E	N	T	R	A	N	T	S

31

A	C	T	S		D	A	N	D	R	U	F	F
P		R		S		D		E		P		U
P	L	A	N	T	E	D		C	A	S	E	S
L		M		R		U		L		I		E
A	P	P	R	O	A	C	H	A	B	L	E	
U				N		E		R		O		S
S	A	V	A	G	E		L	A	U	N	C	H
E		I		W		S		T				E
	R	E	D	I	S	T	R	I	B	U	T	E
A		T		L		A		O		S		P
F	I	N	A	L		P	U	N	C	H	E	D
A		A		E		L		S		E		O
R	E	M	E	D	I	E	S		B	R	I	G

32

C	U	B	I	S	M		A		U		S	
O		U			A	C	T	I	N	I	U	M
M	A	Y			R		H		I		P	
E		I	C	I	C	L	E		V	I	E	W
T		N			H		I		E		R	
S	O	G	G	Y		A	S	C	R	I	B	E
			Y		A		T		S			
C	A	P	R	I	C	E		B	E	F	I	T
	V		A		Q		H			O		R
Z	E	S	T		U	S	U	R	E	R		O
	N		I		I		R			B	O	W
A	U	T	O	C	R	A	T			I		E
	E		N		E		S	A	N	D	A	L

33

U	S	E	D		E	T	H	I	O	P	I	A
N		L		R		R		R		R		N
P	H	O	N	E	M	E		R	O	O	S	T
R		P		S		N		E		D		I
E	V	E	R	T		D	I	S	T	U	R	B
C				A		Y		P		C		A
E	X	O	D	U	S		H	E	C	T	I	C
D		N		R		C		C				T
E	Y	E	B	A	L	L		T	A	B	L	E
N		R		T		A		I		R		R
T	R	O	V	E		R	A	V	I	O	L	I
E		U		U		E		E		K		A
D	I	S	C	R	E	T	E		D	E	L	L

34

B	R	I	E	F	I	N	G		C	R	I	B
A		S		I		O				E		A
B	A	S	I	N		T	R	A	M	M	E	L
Y		U		G		I				A		A
		E		E		C	H	I	C	K	E	N
E	N	D	O	R	S	E		N		E		C
C				T				C				E
O		S		I		A	B	A	S	H	E	D
N	O	T	E	P	A	D		P		A		
O		A				D		A		W		S
M	I	N	E	R	A	L		B	R	A	V	E
I		Z				E		L		I		W
C	R	A	B		A	D	H	E	S	I	O	N

35

	C	A	T	C	H	P	H	R	A	S	E	
B		L		O		H		E		U		L
U		M		G	R	O	V	E		G	E	E
D	R	A	I	N		T		L		A		V
G		N		A		O		S	C	R	E	E
E	X	A	C	T	I	N	G					L
R		C		E				L		A		H
I					S	T	R	U	G	G	L	E
G	R	A	F	T		Y		N		I		A
A		G		U		R		C	I	T	E	D
R	U	E		B	E	A	C	H		A		E
S		N		E		N		E		T		D
	S	T	A	R	S	T	U	D	D	E	D	

36

A	R	C	S		H	I	S	P	A	N	I	C
P		H		H		M		E		E		O
P	R	O	V	E	R	B		N	O	W	I	N
R		I		A		I		N		Y		D
E	R	R	E	D		B	E	S	I	E	G	E
H				Q		E		Y		A		S
E	A	R	F	U	L		C	L	E	R	I	C
N		O		A		B		V				E
S	C	O	U	R	G	E		A	D	D	O	N
I		F		T		A		N		I		S
B	A	T	H	E		C	H	I	A	N	T	I
L		O		R		O		A		G		O
E	X	P	O	S	I	N	G		L	O	I	N

37

A	S	S	E	M	B	L	E		P	E	A	R
J		H		E		E		U		L		O
A	B	U	Z	Z		D	E	N	I	A	L	S
R		T		Z				D		T		E
	B	E	L	O	W	T	H	E	B	E	L	T
S		Y		S		E		T				T
T	I	E		O	U	N	C	E		P	I	E
U				P		S		C		R		S
R	E	S	U	R	R	E	C	T	I	O	N	
G		I		A				A		G		V
E	N	D	I	N	G	S		B	A	R	G	E
O		L		O		I		L		A		E
N	E	E	D		S	T	R	E	A	M	E	R

38

A	L	F	R	E	S	C	O		C	L	U	E
D		I		X		O		C		O		M
M	I	X	U	P		P	E	R	T	U	R	B
I		T		E		I		O		S		E
N	E	U	T	R	O	N		S	W	E	L	L
I		R		I		G		S				L
S	H	E	K	E	L		A	S	S	I	S	I
T				N		A		E		K		S
R	I	V	E	T		M	A	C	B	E	T	H
A		I		I		B		T		B		M
T	R	A	V	A	I	L		I	R	A	T	E
O		L		L		E		O		N		N
R	O	S	E		T	R	A	N	S	A	C	T

39

C	A	N	S		S	T	U	F	F	I	N	G
O		O		N		H		O		M		O
N	I	T	R	A	T	E		R	O	M	E	O
S		E		R		N		M		E		D
C	I	D	E	R		C	H	A	G	R	I	N
I				O		E		L		S		A
O	T	T	A	W	A		A	D	V	E	N	T
U		U		M		U		E				U
S	I	N	K	I	N	G		H	E	W	E	R
N		I		N		L		Y		A		E
E	A	S	E	D		I	N	D	E	X	E	D
S		I		E		E		E		E		L
S	T	A	N	D	A	R	D		E	N	V	Y

40

	A	G	G	R	A	V	A	T	I	N	G	
B		I		I		O		O		U		C
R	E	V		F	E	L	O	N		M		R
I		E		T		U		N	E	E	D	Y
L	A	S	T	S		M		A		R		P
L					S	E	R	G	E	A	N	T
I		T		B				E		L		I
A	D	O	R	A	B	L	E					C
N		B		B		A		M	O	C	H	A
T	O	A	D	Y		C		E		L		L
L		C		S	C	U	B	A		A	L	L
Y		C		I		N		N		S		Y
	P	O	R	T	R	A	I	T	I	S	T	

41

	P		W		A		S	T	R	A	Y	S
C	O	L	O	S	S	A	L			S		U
	S		R		S		A			C	A	B
M	E	E	K		I	M	P	O	S	E		W
	U		E		G		S			N		A
T	R	A	D	I	N	G		J	E	T	T	Y
			U		S		U		V			
L	E	A	P	S		U	N	H	A	P	P	Y
A		B			D		C		N		O	
P		A	M	O	R	A	L		E	E	L	S
P	I	T			O		O		S		I	
E		E			S	C	A	R	C	I	T	Y
D	I	S	H	E	S		K		E		E	

42

D	A	M	P		G	O	L	D	F	I	S	H
I		A		D		C		E		G		A
S	T	Y	L	I	S	T		C	A	N	A	L
T		O		S		A		O		I		F
A	I	R		A		V		M	A	T	C	H
S				G	L	E	A	M		E		E
T		M		R				I		D		A
E		A		E	M	I	T	S				R
F	O	R	C	E		N		S		C	U	T
U		I		M		L		I		E		E
L	A	T	T	E		A	V	O	I	D	E	D
L		A		N		N		N		A		L
Y	U	L	E	T	I	D	E		X	R	A	Y

43

	T	R	U	S	T	W	O	R	T	H	Y	
T		E		I		O		A		Y		A
R		P		D	R	E	A	D		M	A	P
A	G	A	P	E		F		A		N		P
N		S		C		U		R	I	S	E	R
S	A	T	I	A	B	L	E					E
L		S		R				S		B		C
U					P	A	S	T	R	A	M	I
C	A	B	I	N		V		A		H		A
E		A		O		O		T	H	R	O	B
N	U	N		B	O	W	I	E		A		L
T		J		L		A		L		I		E
	R	O	L	E	P	L	A	Y	I	N	G	

44

D	E	T	E	C	T		E		C		D	
I		O			R	O	L	L	O	V	E	R
F	O	X			I		I		N		C	
F		I	C	E	B	O	X		C	R	A	G
E		N			E		I		E		Y	
R	U	S	T	Y		A	R	M	R	E	S	T
			U		A		S		T			
P	E	R	S	O	N	S		V	O	G	U	E
	Q		S		G		E			E		X
P	U	L	L		E	U	L	O	G	Y		U
	I		I		L		E			S	A	D
S	T	I	N	K	I	N	G			E		E
	Y		G		C		Y	E	A	R	N	S

45

H	O	C	K		S	P	E	C	I	F	I	C
O		L		B		O		O		L		A
G	L	U	C	O	S	E		N	O	O	K	S
S		N		I		T		T		W		T
H	I	G	H	S	P	I	R	I	T	E	D	
E				T		C		N		R		F
A	R	M	I	E	S		B	U	R	S	A	R
D		I		R		S		A				I
	I	N	C	O	M	P	A	T	I	B	L	E
F		D		U		R		I		O		N
L	I	F	T	S		A	D	O	P	T	E	D
E		U		L		I		N		C		L
A	L	L	A	Y	I	N	G		W	H	E	Y

46

P	L	A	Y	T	I	M	E		B	E	A	D
R		I		I		U		D		N		O
E	G	R	E	T		S	H	I	A	T	S	U
M		S		T		I		F		E		B
E	C	H	E	L	O	N		F	E	R	A	L
D		I		E		G		I				E
I	N	P	U	T	S		A	C	E	T	I	C
T				A		O		U		R		R
A	V	E	R	T		V	O	L	C	A	N	O
T		A		T		E		T		P		S
I	N	S	U	L	A	R		I	T	E	M	S
O		E		E		D		E		Z		E
N	I	L	E		F	O	R	S	W	E	A	R

47

	P	E	R	S	E	C	U	T	I	O	N	
R		R		M		L		R		L		D
E		A		A	M	I	T	Y		D	U	E
V	E	S	T	S		C		S		E		N
E		I		H		H		T	O	R	S	O
R	E	N	D	E	R	E	D					M
E		G		D				G		L		I
N					E	M	U	L	S	I	O	N
T	U	T	O	R		E		I		M		A
I		A		A		T		D	E	P	O	T
A	S	K		P	U	R	E	E		O		O
L		E		I		I		R		P		R
	P	R	E	D	E	C	E	S	S	O	R	

48

I	N	D	I	R	E	C	T		S	T	O	P
F		O		I		R		S		A		L
F	O	L	I	O		U	N	H	I	N	G	E
Y		P		D		M		A		G		A
	W	H	E	E	L	B	A	R	R	O	W	S
C		I		J		S		P				U
H	A	N	G	A	R		I	S	O	B	A	R
I				N		E		H		E		E
P	R	O	F	E	S	S	I	O	N	A	L	
M		D		I		C		O		R		F
U	N	D	E	R	G	O		T	R	I	L	L
N		L		O		R		E		S		A
K	E	Y	S		S	T	A	R	S	H	I	P

49

■	O	U	T	O	F	B	O	U	N	D	S	■
R	■	N	■	U	■	O	■	R	■	E	■	S
E	■	Q	■	S	L	A	N	G	■	N	E	E
M	O	U	N	T	■	S	■	E	■	S	■	L
E	■	I	■	I	■	T	■	S	H	E	A	F
M	E	E	K	N	E	S	S	■	■	■	■	A
B	■	T	■	G	■	■	■	B	■	T	■	S
R	■	■	■	■	E	N	O	R	M	O	U	S
A	W	F	U	L	■	U	■	E	■	U	■	U
N	■	E	■	A	■	C	■	A	U	G	E	R
C	O	T	■	S	O	L	I	D	■	H	■	E
E	■	E	■	S	■	E	■	T	■	E	■	D
■	A	S	T	O	N	I	S	H	I	N	G	■

50

R	U	E	D	■	U	N	A	W	A	R	E	S
E	■	V	■	R	■	I	■	E	■	E	■	I
C	L	O	S	E	U	P	■	L	A	D	E	N
E	■	K	■	A	■	■	■	T	■	U	■	E
I	N	E	X	P	E	R	I	E	N	C	E	■
V	■	■	■	P	■	O	■	R	■	E	■	O
E	R	R	■	E	L	B	O	W	■	S	O	B
D	■	A	■	A	■	E	■	E	■	■	■	S
■	O	V	E	R	E	S	T	I	M	A	T	E
S	■	I	■	A	■	■	■	G	■	O	■	S
L	I	N	E	N	■	E	X	H	O	R	T	S
A	■	E	■	C	■	A	■	T	■	T	■	E
M	A	S	S	E	U	R	S	■	H	A	N	D

51

■	U	T	I	L	I	T	A	R	I	A	N	■
K	■	O	■	O	■	A	■	E	■	S	■	E
I	R	K	■	B	I	S	O	N	■	S	■	L
N	■	E	■	B	■	T	■	E	L	U	D	E
D	A	N	D	Y	■	E	■	W	■	R	■	C
H	■	■	■	■	A	D	J	A	C	E	N	T
E	■	S	■	T	■	■	■	L	■	S	■	R
A	P	I	A	R	I	S	T	■	■	■	■	O
R	■	L	■	U	■	O	■	S	H	O	W	N
T	E	E	N	S	■	D	■	E	■	P	■	I
E	■	N	■	T	R	I	A	D	■	A	R	C
D	■	C	■	E	■	U	■	A	■	L	■	S
■	D	E	T	E	R	M	I	N	I	S	M	■

52

C	A	S	H	■	R	E	A	B	S	O	R	B
O	■	K	■	D	■	U	■	R	■	R	■	O
N	O	I	S	I	E	R	■	A	D	I	E	U
C	■	R	■	S	■	O	■	I	■	G	■	I
E	X	T	R	A	■	P	I	N	B	A	L	L
N	■	■	■	D	■	E	■	W	■	M	■	L
T	H	R	I	V	E	■	M	A	R	I	N	A
R	■	O	■	A	■	L	■	S	■	■	■	B
A	T	L	A	N	T	A	■	H	Y	D	R	A
T	■	L	■	T	■	N	■	I	■	O	■	I
I	B	I	Z	A	■	C	O	N	C	U	R	S
O	■	N	■	G	■	E	■	G	■	G	■	S
N	E	G	L	E	C	T	S	■	S	H	O	E

53

R	A	C	C	O	O	N	S	■	L	A	I	D
E	■	O	■	L	■	E	■	P	■	R	■	I
I	N	L	A	Y	■	V	I	R	U	S	E	S
N	■	L	■	M	■	A	■	I	■	O	■	C
C	H	O	P	P	E	D	■	D	O	N	O	R
A	■	I	■	I	■	A	■	E	■	■	■	E
R	E	D	U	C	E	■	R	O	O	T	E	D
N	■	■	■	G	■	B	■	F	■	W	■	I
A	R	O	M	A	■	A	P	P	O	I	N	T
T	■	I	■	M	■	S	■	L	■	R	■	A
I	L	L	N	E	S	S	■	A	D	L	I	B
O	■	E	■	S	■	E	■	C	■	E	■	L
N	O	D	S	■	A	T	T	E	N	D	E	E

54

L	U	S	H	■	C	A	P	S	I	C	U	M
A	■	P	■	A	■	N	■	H	■	O	■	O
B	O	O	T	L	E	G	■	O	W	N	E	D
R	■	O	■	P	■	E	■	R	■	C	■	E
A	N	N	I	H	I	L	A	T	I	O	N	■
D	■	■	■	A	■	S	■	C	■	C	■	E
O	R	I	E	N	T	■	S	H	U	T	U	P
R	■	N	■	U	■	P	■	A	■	■	■	I
■	C	H	A	M	P	I	O	N	S	H	I	P
S	■	A	■	E	■	N	■	G	■	A	■	H
P	O	L	A	R	■	I	N	E	R	T	I	A
A	■	E	■	I	■	O	■	D	■	E	■	N
R	E	D	U	C	I	N	G	■	I	D	L	Y

55

	N		E		A		D	E	R	A	I	L
P	O	S	S	I	B	L	E			L		U
	O		P		R		C			W	A	X
E	D	G	E		A	Z	A	L	E	A		U
	L		C		D		Y			Y		R
R	E	S	I	D	E	S		P	E	S	K	Y
			A		S		S		U			
H	U	L	L	S		C	U	R	R	I	E	S
E		O			H		M		O		M	
C		A	U	R	O	R	A		P	R	I	G
K	I	N			U		T		E		N	
L		E			N	A	R	R	A	T	E	S
E	R	R	A	N	D		A		N		M	

56

S	U	M	O		P	I	E	R	C	I	N	G
T		U		C		C		E		R		R
A	B	S	O	L	V	E		A	M	I	G	O
N		I		E				S		D		W
D	I	C	T	A	T	O	R	S	H	I	P	
O				R		M		E		U		E
F	O	E		S	E	E	R	S		M	A	D
F		P		I		G		S				U
	D	I	A	G	R	A	M	M	A	T	I	C
A		S		H				E		H		A
S	N	O	U	T		C	O	N	V	E	R	T
I		D		E		A		T		R		E
A	M	E	N	D	I	N	G		D	E	E	D

57

H	O	S	T		P	U	G	I	L	I	S	M
A		U		O		N		M		M		O
R	A	D	I	C	A	L		P	O	P	U	P
D		A		C		I		E		O		E
C	A	N	T	A	N	K	E	R	O	U	S	
O				S		E		T		N		P
P	R	E	L	I	M		G	I	R	D	E	R
Y		M		O		F		N				O
	C	O	I	N	C	I	D	E	N	T	A	L
U		T		A		N		N		R		O
T	W	I	R	L		I	T	C	H	I	N	G
A		O		L		T		E		T		U
H	O	N	E	Y	B	E	E		M	E	T	E

58

	R	E	C	O	N	S	T	R	U	C	T	
A		V		B		U		E		A		S
R		O		V	O	L	G	A		S	L	Y
M	E	L	E	E		L		R		E		N
E		V		R		E		M	E	D	I	C
D	R	E	S	S	I	N	G					H
F		S		E				S		B		R
O					V	I	R	T	U	O	S	O
R	U	G	B	Y		N		I		T		N
C		A		E		D		P	I	A	N	O
E	L	M		A	D	O	R	E		N		U
S		M		R		O		N		I		S
	M	A	S	S	P	R	O	D	U	C	E	

59

S	A	L	O	N	S		P		V		P	
I		E			W	A	S	T	E	F	U	L
G	Y	M			E		Y		R		F	
N		M	O	S	A	I	C		T	I	F	F
E		A			T		H		E		I	
D	U	S	T	S		F	I	B	B	I	N	G
			R		S		C		R			
R	A	D	I	C	L	E		C	A	C	H	E
	M		P		A		S			O		L
G	A	L	L		N	E	P	H	E	W		I
	Z		I		T		O			B	O	X
D	O	W	N	B	E	A	T			O		I
	N		G		D		S	A	W	Y	E	R

60

W	I	L	L		S	C	O	R	C	H	E	S
O		A		S		R		E		I		E
R	E	C	L	U	S	E		P	E	T	A	L
D		E		R		D		E		T		F
P	A	D		R		I		R	A	I	S	E
R				O	P	T	I	C		N		V
O		R		U				U		G		I
C		E		N	I	C	K	S				D
E	N	D	E	D		O		S		B	E	E
S		N		I		B		I		L		N
S	T	E	R	N		B	U	O	Y	A	N	T
O		S		G		L		N		Z		L
R	E	S	I	S	T	E	D		L	E	V	Y

61

W	A	R	R	A	N	T	Y		J	A	V	A
A		U		S		E		C		P		W
Y	A	C	H	T		S	T	A	M	I	N	A
S		T		R		T		B		A		K
	D	I	S	O	B	E	D	I	E	N	C	E
A		O		L		D		N				N
S	E	N	I	O	R		R	E	S	C	U	E
P				G		A		T		O		D
I	N	F	R	I	N	G	E	M	E	N	T	
R		R		C		L		A		C		P
I	T	E	R	A	T	E		K	N	E	L	L
N		E		L		A		E		A		E
G	O	D	S		U	M	B	R	E	L	L	A

62

U	G	L	Y		E	S	C	A	P	I	N	G
N		O		P		I		C		N		O
I	N	V	E	R	S	E		C	A	R	O	L
N		E		E		S		E		O		D
H	A	D		S		T		L	E	A	S	E
A				U	S	A	G	E		D		N
B		P		M				R		S		J
I		R		P	A	S	T	A				U
T	R	O	U	T		T		T		M	O	B
A		S		U		R		I		I		I
B	R	A	V	O		A	R	O	U	S	A	L
L		I		U		I		N		T		E
E	X	C	U	S	I	N	G		I	S	L	E

63

	I	L	L	T	E	M	P	E	R	E	D	
D		I		O		E		P		X		D
O	A	K		T	U	N	E	S		P		I
U		E		E		A		I	R	O	N	S
B	E	D	I	M		C		L		R		G
L					R	E	P	O	R	T	E	R
E		B		A				N		S		A
F	O	R	E	M	O	S	T					C
A		O		A		C		L	U	C	R	E
U	N	T	I	L		R		U		H		F
L		H		G	L	O	O	M		E	M	U
T		E		A		L		E		S		L
	C	R	U	M	B	L	I	N	E	S	S	

64

D	O	S	E		C	E	L	E	R	I	A	C
I		C		S		R		M		M		O
S	T	A	T	U	E	S		B	R	A	W	N
T		L		B		A		A		G		G
I	N	P	U	T		T	E	R	R	I	E	R
N				E		Z		R		N		E
C	A	P	E	R	S		W	A	K	E	N	S
T		A		R		S		S				S
I	M	P	E	A	C	H		S	C	R	E	W
V		R		N		A		I		I		O
E	X	I	L	E		K	I	N	G	D	O	M
L		K		A		E		G		G		A
Y	E	A	R	N	I	N	G		M	E	A	N

65

D	E	P	O	T	S		P		H		P	
O		R			T	R	I	C	Y	C	L	E
W	O	O			I		R		S		A	
S		P	A	E	L	L	A		T	R	I	M
E		E			L		N		E		C	
R	E	L	A	X		S	H	O	R	T	E	N
			S		R		A		I			
H	A	M	S	T	E	R		J	A	P	A	N
	V		O		A		G			E		E
H	A	I	R		S	C	A	R	A	B		A
	T		T		O		L			B	U	T
P	A	T	E	R	N	A	L			L		E
	R		D		S		S	T	R	E	W	N

66

Q	U	A	Y		B	A	T	H	R	O	O	M
U		L		D		T		A		B		O
A	I	L	M	E	N	T		I	N	L	E	T
D		A		L		E		R		O		H
R	A	Y		I		S		D	A	N	C	E
I				Q	A	T	A	R		G		R
L		S		U				E		S		C
A		U		E	L	V	E	S				O
T	U	B	E	S		O		S		T	A	U
E		U		C		I		I		R		N
R	A	N	G	E		C	O	N	T	O	R	T
A		I		N		E		G		L		R
L	A	T	I	T	U	D	E		P	L	O	Y

67

M	I	S	S	O	U	R	I		C	L	I	P
A		H		V		U		U		Y		A
R	O	U	T	E		T	E	N	D	R	I	L
S		T		R				S		I		I
	C	O	N	S	E	Q	U	E	N	C	E	S
V		F		I		U		A				A
O	A	F		M	E	A	L	S		A	D	D
L				P		R		O		S		E
C	O	M	P	L	E	T	E	N	E	S	S	
A		E		I				A		A		T
N	E	E	D	F	U	L		B	O	U	G	H
I		T		Y		A		L		L		U
C	U	S	P		O	B	J	E	C	T	E	D

68

S	U	D	S		A	C	O	U	S	T	I	C
L		I		C		O		N		Y		R
E	N	G	U	L	F	S		R	O	C	K	Y
I		I		O		I		E		O		P
G	O	T		T		N		A	L	O	F	T
H				H	E	E	D	S		N		O
T		S		E				O		S		G
O		W		S	E	V	E	N				R
F	A	I	T	H		I		A		B	O	A
H		F		O		A		B		E		P
A	S	T	E	R		B	U	L	L	I	S	H
N		E		S		L		E		N		E
D	A	R	K	E	N	E	D		A	G	A	R

69

	E	L	A	B	O	R	A	T	E	L	Y	
G		I		E		U		U		O		T
R	I	M		T	A	S	T	E		G		E
E		I		E		S		S	O	B	E	R
E	X	T	O	L		I		D		O		M
N					M	A	C	A	R	O	N	I
H		E		A				Y		K		N
O	R	G	A	N	I	S	M					O
U		O		O		A		L	A	P	E	L
S	A	T	E	D		V		A		Y		O
E		I		Y	E	A	S	T		L	E	G
S		S		N		N		I		O		Y
	I	M	P	E	R	T	I	N	E	N	T	

70

L	I	G	H	T	S		D		R		B	
A		A			W	H	I	T	E	H	O	T
D	U	G			A		V		P		A	
L		G	O	B	B	L	E		A	C	R	E
E		L			S		R		R		D	
S	H	E	L	L		E	G	O	T	I	S	T
			I		U		E		E			
S	T	A	G	I	N	G		Y	E	A	R	N
	A		N		C		P			C		I
F	L	U	E		I	T	A	L	I	C		M
	E		O		V		N			R	U	B
E	N	D	U	R	I	N	G			U		L
	T		S		L		S	P	E	E	D	Y

71

C	U	L	T	U	R	A	L		V	E	A	L
O		I		N		S		S		R		O
S	O	F	I	A		S	U	C	C	U	M	B
T		T		N		I		R		P		B
	C	O	N	S	I	S	T	E	N	T	L	Y
O		F		W		T		E				I
B	U	F	F	E	T		A	N	N	U	L	S
T				R		T		W		M		T
A	R	O	M	A	T	H	E	R	A	P	Y	
I		U		B		E		I		I		H
N	E	S	T	L	E	S		T	E	R	S	E
E		T		E		E		E		E		R
D	U	S	T		E	S	P	R	E	S	S	O

72

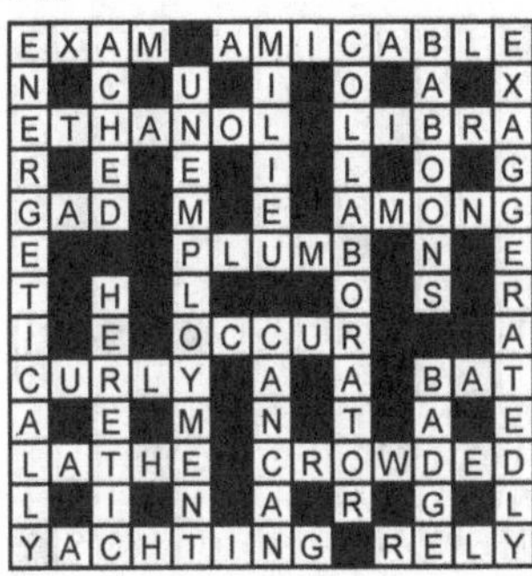

E	X	A	M		A	M	I	C	A	B	L	E
N		C		U		I		O		A		X
E	T	H	A	N	O	L		L	I	B	R	A
R		E		E		I		L		O		G
G	A	D		M		E		A	M	O	N	G
E				P	L	U	M	B		N		E
T		H		L				O		S		R
I		E		O	C	C	U	R				A
C	U	R	L	Y		A		A		B	A	T
A		E		M		N		T		A		E
L	A	T	H	E		C	R	O	W	D	E	D
L		I		N		A		R		G		L
Y	A	C	H	T	I	N	G		R	E	L	Y

73

D	U	C	K		S	T	O	P	P	A	G	E
A		R		R		E		E		R		A
F	R	E	S	H	E	N		R	I	S	K	S
T		A		O		S		S		E		T
N	A	M	E	D	R	O	P	P	I	N	G	
E				O		R		I		I		P
S	T	R	I	D	E		A	C	A	C	I	A
S		E		E		O		A				L
	M	A	G	N	I	F	I	C	E	N	C	E
W		C		D		F		I		O		T
O	U	T	E	R		E	N	T	R	U	S	T
O		O		O		R		Y		N		E
F	I	R	M	N	E	S	S		A	S	K	S

74

75

P	O	D	S		P	A	R	A	F	F	I	N
E		E		I		C		L		O		O
C	A	B	I	N	E	T		L	Y	R	E	S
T		T		S				I		E		Y
O	B	S	C	U	R	A	N	T	I	S	M	
R				F		T		E		E		R
A	M	P		F	L	O	U	R		E	Y	E
L		E		I		N		A				V
	U	N	A	C	C	E	P	T	A	B	L	E
C		G		I				I		E		R
H	O	U	S	E		N	O	O	D	L	E	S
I		I		N		A		N		O		E
C	E	N	O	T	A	P	H		T	W	O	S

76

77

	S	U	B	S	I	S	T	E	N	C	E	
N		N		U		A		Y		H		C
O	A	T		R	I	F	L	E		E		A
N		I		G		A		L	O	V	E	R
P	I	E	C	E		R		E		R		D
A					V	I	R	T	U	O	S	I
R		E		C				S		N		O
T	E	M	P	O	R	A	L					G
I		A		P		P		S	T	A	I	R
S	U	N	N	Y		P		H		S		A
A		A		C	R	E	D	O		H	I	P
N		T		A		A		A		E		H
	F	E	A	T	U	R	E	L	E	S	S	

78

S	C	U	D		D	I	T	H	E	R	E	D
I		R		P		C		Y		I		E
L	I	B	E	R	I	A		P	R	O	O	F
V		A		A		R		O		T		E
E	N	N	U	I		U	N	C	L	E	A	R
R				S		S		H		R		E
J	A	M	M	E	D		W	O	R	S	E	N
U		E		W		L		N				T
B	E	S	P	O	K	E		D	U	B	A	I
I		S		R		P		R		U		A
L	E	A	S	T		T	R	I	V	I	A	L
E		G		H		O		A		L		L
E	V	E	R	Y	O	N	E		E	D	D	Y

79

M	I	F	F		E	X	E	C	U	T	O	R
I		L		O		E		O		R		A
S	T	O	P	P	E	R		N	E	E	D	S
T		P		P		X		T		A		P
R	E	S	E	R	V	E	P	R	I	C	E	
E				E		S		A		L		P
A	M	I	D	S	T		A	D	H	E	R	E
T		N		S		A		I				N
	D	I	S	I	N	F	E	C	T	A	N	T
S		T		V		R		T		M		A
A	F	I	R	E		I	C	E	B	E	R	G
G		A		L		C		D		N		O
A	L	L	E	Y	W	A	Y		E	D	E	N

80

B	A	C	K		C	H	U	T	Z	P	A	H
E		A		B		O		R		O		E
T	U	R	N	I	N	G		A	N	N	U	L
R		E		O				N		T		P
A	N	T	A	G	O	N	I	S	T	I	C	
Y				R		E		F		F		H
A	U	K		A	W	A	R	E		F	R	Y
L		I		P		R		R				A
	E	N	T	H	U	S	I	A	S	T	I	C
S		S		I				B		I		I
C	O	M	I	C		H	A	L	O	G	E	N
A		A		A		A		E		H		T
M	I	N	D	L	E	S	S		I	T	C	H

81

C	A	S	E		B	U	D	D	H	I	S	M
H		A		C		N		I		N		E
A	N	I	M	A	L	S		S	T	E	E	D
R		N		T		U		B		X		I
A	N	T		A		R		E	X	A	L	T
C				S	P	E	L	L		C		E
T		L		T				I		T		R
E		I		R	E	U	S	E				R
R	A	T	I	O		N		V		L	E	A
L		E		P		C		I		O		N
E	A	R	T	H		L	I	N	E	A	G	E
S		A		I		E		G		C		A
S	O	L	E	C	I	S	M		C	H	I	N

82

C	O	C	K	C	R	O	W		E	L	M	S
O		O		H		C		S		U		E
M	I	N	E	R		T	O	P	I	C	A	L
P		T		I		A		I		I		F
L	I	A	I	S	O	N		C	O	D	E	R
I		I		T		T		K				I
M	A	N	A	M	A		F	A	C	I	N	G
E				A		H		N		C		H
N	E	C	K	S		O	D	D	M	E	N	T
T		I		E		L		S		C		E
A	R	R	I	V	A	L		P	H	O	T	O
R		C		E		E		A		L		U
Y	U	A	N		G	R	E	N	A	D	E	S

83

F	R	E	Q	U	E	N	T		A	C	M	E
I		N		N		E		I		A		A
V	I	S	T	A		A	W	N	I	N	G	S
E		U		T		R		T		O		T
	P	R	O	T	U	B	E	R	A	N	C	E
E		E		A		Y		A				R
M	A	S	T	I	C		U	N	R	E	A	L
B				N		N		S		V		Y
A	L	P	H	A	B	E	T	I	C	A	L	
T		A		B		E		G		S		S
T	O	P	P	L	E	D		E	V	I	C	T
L		E		E		L		N		V		E
E	U	R	O		S	E	A	T	B	E	L	T

84

B	A	C	C	A	R	A	T		S	U	R	F
U		O		P		B		Q		M		A
S	L	U	M	P		B	O	U	R	B	O	N
I		N		R		E		E		E		T
N	U	C	L	E	U	S		S	Y	R	I	A
E		I		H		S		T				S
S	A	L	T	E	D		M	I	N	U	E	T
S				N		U		O		P		I
W	A	D	E	S		G	E	N	E	R	I	C
O		U		I		A		A		I		A
M	O	N	S	O	O	N		B	A	G	E	L
A		E		N		D		L		H		L
N	E	S	T		T	A	P	E	S	T	R	Y

85

S	I	D	E	K	I	C	K		A	G	E	D
U		O		I		O		C		L		I
N	A	S	A	L		L	O	O	S	E	N	S
S		S		L		D		N		A		P
	L	I	F	E	S	E	N	T	E	N	C	E
E		E		R		R		E				R
S	T	R	A	W	S		S	M	O	C	K	S
P				H		C		P		H		E
O	N	O	M	A	T	O	P	O	E	I	A	
U		V		L		M		R		C		B
S	H	A	K	E	U	P		A	W	A	K	E
A		L		S		E		R		G		A
L	A	S	H		P	L	A	Y	R	O	O	M

86

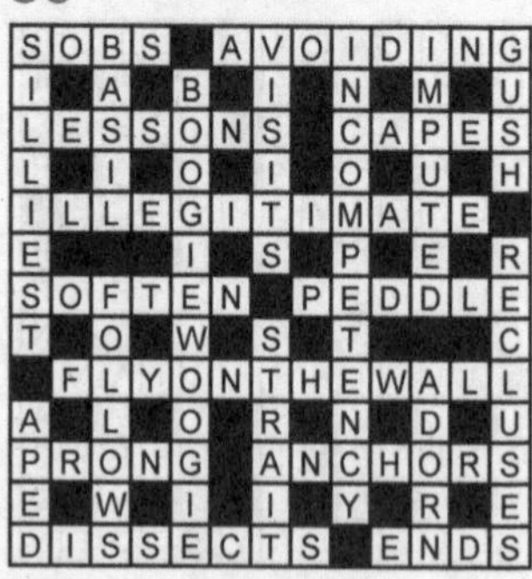

87

S	H	A	B	B	I	L	Y		A	W	E	D
A		U		A		O		I		A		I
R	E	S	I	N		W	I	N	D	I	N	G
I		T		T				T		V		E
	C	R	E	A	T	I	V	E	N	E	S	S
C		I		M		D		L				T
R	I	A		W	H	E	E	L		B	Y	E
U				E		A		I		A		D
C	A	R	D	I	O	L	O	G	I	S	T	
I		E		G				I		S		E
B	E	A	R	H	U	G		B	L	O	O	M
L		C		T		N		L		O		M
E	A	T	S		B	U	O	Y	A	N	C	Y

88

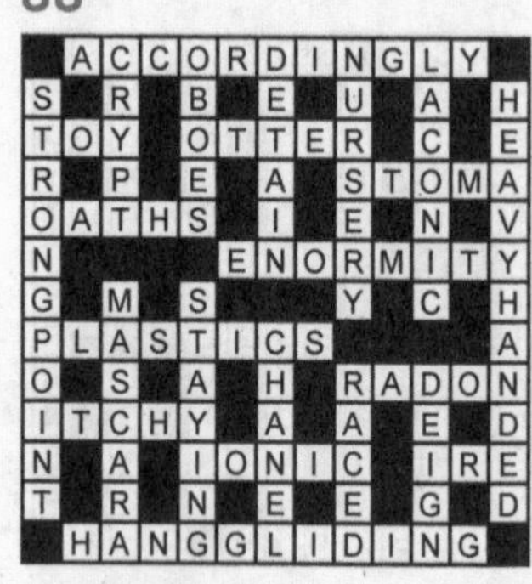

89

B	O	D	Y		H	I	G	H	B	R	O	W
R		A		I		N		O		A		H
A	T	T	E	M	P	T		U	N	I	F	Y
N		E		P		E		S		D		S
D	I	S	H	E	A	R	T	E	N	E	D	
I				R		N		K		R		A
S	C	H	I	S	T		M	E	S	S	U	P
H		U		O		P		E				P
	F	R	O	N	T	I	S	P	I	E	C	E
C		T		A		E		I		I		A
H	O	I	S	T		R	E	N	E	G	E	S
A		N		O		C		G		H		E
R	E	G	A	R	D	E	D		S	T	I	R

90

A	N	N	O	U	N	C	E		M	E	N	U
L		A		N		A		U		A		N
P	A	R	E	D		S	A	N	G	R	I	A
H		W		E		I		O		L		D
A	B	H	O	R		N		F		Y	O	U
A		A		A	L	O	O	F				L
N		L		C				I		A		T
D				H	A	V	O	C		L		E
O	R	B		I		I		I	D	L	E	R
M		E		E		E		A		E		A
E	N	L	I	V	E	N		L	I	G	H	T
G		L		E		N		L		R		E
A	V	E	R		B	A	B	Y	H	O	O	D

91

B	E	F	U	D	D	L	E		T	O	Y	S
U		I		I		O				N		I
N	I	C	E	R		U	N	C	L	E	A	N
T		K		E		V				W		I
		L		C		R	E	P	L	A	Y	S
T	R	E	S	T	L	E		E		Y		T
H				I				A				E
E		S		N		I	N	C	I	S	O	R
O	C	T	A	G	O	N		E		L		
R		O				F		A		A		V
E	N	D	G	A	M	E		B	E	L	I	E
M		G				R		L		O		N
S	E	E	M		E	S	T	E	E	M	E	D

92

G	E	L	S		A	M	I	C	A	B	L	Y
A		O		M		R		A		L		A
Z	I	G	Z	A	G	S		P	L	U	C	K
P		I		N				I		R		S
A	R	C	H	I	T	E	C	T	U	R	E	
C				P		X		U		E		U
H	E	M		U	S	U	A	L		D	E	N
O		A		L		L		A				D
	B	R	E	A	S	T	S	T	R	O	K	E
T		I		T				I		R		R
H	A	N	O	I		W	R	O	N	G	E	D
O		E		O		A		N		A		O
R	A	R	E	N	E	S	S		S	N	A	G

93

	A	S	S	O	C	I	A	T	I	O	N	
S		L		T		R		U		B		C
T	O	E		H	O	O	K	S		V		H
O		E		E		N		S	P	I	K	E
M	A	K	E	R		E		O		A		E
A					E	D	U	C	A	T	E	S
C		O		D				K		E		E
H	A	R	V	E	S	T	S					C
A		G		S		Y		C	A	M	E	L
C	H	A	L	K		C		L		A		O
H		N		T	R	O	P	E		J	U	T
E		I		O		O		A		O		H
	A	C	U	P	U	N	C	T	U	R	E	

94

F	U	S	S		F	A	N	D	A	N	G	O
E		Q		I		D		I		E		V
A	L	U	M	N	U	S		S	H	A	V	E
T		I		T		O		C		T		R
H	O	B		E		R		O	V	E	N	S
E				R	O	B	I	N		S		T
R		V		M				N		T		A
W		I		E	T	U	D	E				T
E	B	B	E	D		P		C		T	H	E
I		R		I		T		T		H		M
G	U	A	V	A		A	P	E	L	I	K	E
H		N		T		K		D		R		N
T	O	T	T	E	R	E	D		E	D	I	T

95

T	A	C	K		E	C	L	I	P	S	E	S
R		U		O		O		N		T		H
E	M	B	A	S	S	Y		V	I	O	L	A
M		I		T				U		P		M
B	A	C	T	E	R	I	O	L	O	G	Y	
L				N		D		N		A		S
E	N	D		T	H	E	S	E		P	A	P
D		E		A		A		R				O
	O	L	D	T	E	S	T	A	M	E	N	T
A		I		I				B		D		L
L	I	M	B	O		C	U	L	T	U	R	E
A		I		U		O		E		C		S
S	E	T	A	S	I	D	E		T	E	E	S

96

	C	A	T	A	S	T	R	O	P	H	E	
I		N		T		O		X		U		I
L		D		T	H	U	M	B		M	U	M
L	A	R	G	E		P		O		P		M
U		O		N		E		W	A	S	T	E
S	K	I	N	D	E	E	P					D
T		D		S				C		S		I
R					P	A	N	O	R	A	M	A
A	L	T	A	R		L		U		L		T
T		W		E		M		N	O	V	A	E
E	W	E		C	O	O	K	S		A		L
D		E		U		S		E		G		Y
	S	T	O	R	Y	T	E	L	L	E	R	

97

I	N	K	S		O	M	I	S	S	I	O	N
N		I		S		E		H		N		O
T	R	O	T	T	E	D		A	G	A	I	N
R		S		R		I		R		N		A
A	R	K		A		U		P	O	I	N	T
N				T	E	M	P	T		T		T
S		P		O				O		Y		E
I		R		S	K	E	I	N				N
G	R	A	S	P		X		G		F	E	D
E		I		H		P		U		A		A
N	O	R	S	E		O	V	E	R	R	A	N
C		I		R		R		D		E		C
E	L	E	M	E	N	T	S		I	D	L	E

98

	A	M	B	A	S	S	A	D	O	R	S	
M		O		S		T		E		H		A
A	I	D		S	T	I	N	G		I		G
C		E		A		G		R	A	Z	O	R
R	A	L	L	Y		M		A		O		I
O					P	A	N	D	E	M	I	C
S		C		K				E		E		U
C	L	A	R	I	N	E	T					L
O		L		N		T		P	I	P	I	T
P	A	Y	E	E		H		I		A		U
I		P		T	W	I	S	T		C	U	R
C		S		I		C		O		T		E
	C	O	N	C	I	S	E	N	E	S	S	

99

	P		A		I		B	E	D	L	A	M
P	E	R	S	O	N	A	L			E		E
	R		S		S		I			S	U	M
G	U	R	U		T	E	N	N	I	S		O
	S		M		E		D			E		R
R	E	V	I	V	A	L		E	N	E	M	Y
			N		D		R		O			
B	I	N	G	O		D	E	T	R	A	C	T
R		O			F		P		T		O	
O		U	R	S	I	N	E		H	U	S	H
K	E	G			X		A		E		M	
E		A			E	X	T	E	R	I	O	R
R	O	T	U	N	D		S		N		S	

100

F	L	A	T	F	I	S	H		S	T	E	M
E		N		R		A		I		R		I
L	L	A	M	A		L	A	R	D	E	R	S
I		L		U		A		R		A		U
C	R	O	W	D		M		E		D	O	N
I		G		U	N	I	T	S				D
T		Y		L				I		M		E
A				E	P	I	C	S		E		R
T	U	B		N		R		T	I	M	E	S
I		L		T		I		I		E		T
O	R	A	C	L	E	S		B	O	N	G	O
N		N		Y		E		L		T		O
S	A	K	E		A	S	T	E	R	O	I	D

101

S	U	B	D	U	E		A		C		B	
E		R			N	U	M	E	R	O	U	S
L	I	E			T		E		I		N	
D		W	A	R	R	E	N		T	R	I	P
O		E			Y		I		E		O	
M	A	R	S	H		S	T	O	R	I	N	G
			T		C		Y		I			
Q	U	I	E	T	L	Y		V	A	L	U	E
	N		A		E		S			O		N
O	V	A	L		R	A	K	I	N	G		Z
	E		T		I		I			J	O	Y
N	I	G	H	T	C	A	P			A		M
	L		Y		S		S	T	Y	M	I	E

102

S	O	M	E		C	L	I	M	A	T	I	C
E		A		I		I		I		R		O
M	E	L	A	N	I	N		S	P	A	W	N
I		T		V		E		A		C		T
C	R	A	T	E		A	U	D	I	T	O	R
O				R		R		V		O		O
N	E	G	A	T	E		H	E	N	R	Y	V
S		A		E		S		N				E
C	A	R	I	B	O	U		T	A	P	E	R
I		N		R		B		U		R		S
O	P	E	R	A		M	A	R	T	I	N	I
U		T		T		I		E		M		A
S	U	S	P	E	C	T	S		W	E	L	L

103

	A	D	V	E	N	T	U	R	O	U	S	
A		O		M		E		E		N		S
F	A	D		P	O	E	T	S		L		M
T		O		T		T		H	Y	E	N	A
E	S	S	A	Y		E		A		A		L
R					P	R	O	P	O	S	A	L
B		G		A				E		H		C
U	G	L	I	N	E	S	S					H
R		I		I		E		R	U	M	B	A
N	A	M	E	S		W		E		E		N
E		P		E	N	A	C	T		L	O	G
R		S		E		G		R		O		E
	N	E	E	D	L	E	P	O	I	N	T	

104

	C	L	I	M	A	T	O	L	O	G	Y	
C		A		I		E		E		A		P
H		T		S	P	A	S	M		P	A	R
L	O	T	U	S		S		M		E		E
O		I		I		E		A	I	D	E	D
R	E	C	E	N	T	L	Y					O
O		E		G				G		L		M
P					K	A	L	A	H	A	R	I
H	O	V	E	R		G		R		U		N
Y		I		I		E		M	E	N	S	A
L	U	X		G	U	I	L	E		D		N
L		E		H		N		N		E		T
	I	N	S	T	I	G	A	T	O	R	S	

105

C	A	N	T		C	R	U	S	A	D	E	R
H		O		T		A		O		E		I
I	N	T	E	R	I	M		M	O	V	E	D
L		E		I		M		N		A		E
D	I	S	A	G	R	E	E	A	B	L	E	
R				O		D		M		U		B
E	X	P	A	N	D		A	B	S	E	I	L
N		R		O		S		U				A
	C	O	S	M	O	P	O	L	I	T	A	N
P		R		E		H		I		U		K
A	P	A	R	T		E	S	S	E	N	C	E
T		T		R		R		M		E		T
H	E	A	V	Y	S	E	T		O	D	E	S

106

D	O	F	F		V	E	R	T	I	C	A	L
O		O		C		R		O		O		O
W	A	R	T	H	O	G		G	A	M	U	T
N		G		E				E		P		S
C	L	O	S	E	M	O	U	T	H	E	D	
A				S		R		H		T		E
S	A	G		E	L	I	T	E		E	E	L
T		I		B		B		R				A
	F	R	E	U	D	I	A	N	S	L	I	P
I		A		R				E		Y		S
B	E	F	O	G		S	A	S	H	I	M	I
I		F		E		I		S		N		N
S	N	E	E	R	I	N	G		A	G	O	G

107

D	I	S	P	R	O	V	E		B	E	E	F
E		C		E		I		Q		N		O
T	H	R	U	M		R	O	U	N	D	E	R
E		A		O		A		I		O		E
R	O	W	E	R		G		N		W	O	K
M		N		S	C	O	U	T				N
I		Y		E				E		G		O
N				F	A	C	E	S		R		W
A	R	T		U		A		S	T	O	O	L
T		E		L		V		E		M		E
I	M	P	U	L	S	E		N	A	M	E	D
O		I		Y		I		C		E		G
N	O	D	E		U	N	S	E	T	T	L	E

108

R	I	M	S		P	R	E	C	E	D	E	S
I		O		I		W		O		E		I
C	A	D	E	N	Z	A		N	A	V	A	L
O		E		V		N		S		I		K
C	O	M	M	E	N	D	A	T	I	O	N	
H				S		A		I		U		A
E	V	I	C	T	S		S	T	A	S	I	S
T		S		I		J		U				S
	C	O	N	G	L	O	M	E	R	A	T	E
B		T		A		Y		N		N		S
A	F	O	O	T		F	A	C	T	O	R	S
L		P		O		U		Y		D		E
D	R	E	A	R	I	L	Y		T	E	N	S

109

C	A	K	E		P	A	T	H	E	T	I	C
O		E		H		U		I		A		H
R	U	B	B	I	N	G		E	A	G	E	R
R		A		N		U		R		G		Y
E	M	B	E	D		S	T	O	R	I	E	S
S				Q		T		G		N		A
P	O	D	I	U	M		F	L	A	G	O	N
O		I		A		B		Y				T
N	O	S	T	R	I	L		P	O	A	C	H
D		D		T		O		H		B		E
I	M	A	G	E		U	N	I	F	O	R	M
N		I		R		S		C		V		U
G	A	N	G	S	T	E	R		H	E	L	M

110

U	N	W	A	N	T	E	D		A	C	H	E
N		H		O		N		D		H		S
P	R	E	E	N		C	U	R	R	E	N	T
R		T		A		O		E		E		A
E	X	H	A	L	E	D		S	H	R	U	B
T		E		C		E		S				L
E	N	R	O	O	T		B	I	K	I	N	I
N				H		C		N		M		S
T	A	B	O	O		A	N	G	U	I	S	H
I		U		L		R		D		T		M
O	R	I	F	I	C	E		O	V	A	T	E
U		L		C		E		W		T		N
S	E	T	S		T	R	A	N	S	E	C	T

111

D	R	U	M	B	E	A	T		I	C	E	D
A		M		L		D		I		U		I
Z	E	B	R	A		O	M	N	I	B	U	S
E		R		B		R		C		E		T
	R	A	B	B	L	E	R	O	U	S	E	R
A		G		E		D		M				E
D	R	E	A	R	Y		O	P	U	S	E	S
M				M		H		E		P		S
I	N	T	R	O	D	U	C	T	I	O	N	
R		A		U		D		E		N		O
E	X	C	I	T	E	D		N	I	G	E	R
R		K		H		L		C		E		A
S	O	S	O		R	E	V	E	R	S	A	L

112

F	O	W	L		S	P	R	I	N	T	E	R
O		O		A		O		N		W		I
R	E	M	O	V	E	S		T	R	E	E	S
E		E		A		I		E		E		K
C	O	N	G	R	A	T	U	L	A	T	E	
A				I		S		L		E		D
S	E	L	E	C	T		F	I	E	R	C	E
T		O		I		A		G				P
	I	N	D	O	C	T	R	I	N	A	T	E
E		G		U		T		B		N		N
L	O	B	E	S		U	N	L	O	V	E	D
A		O		L		N		E		I		E
N	E	W	L	Y	W	E	D		G	L	A	D

113

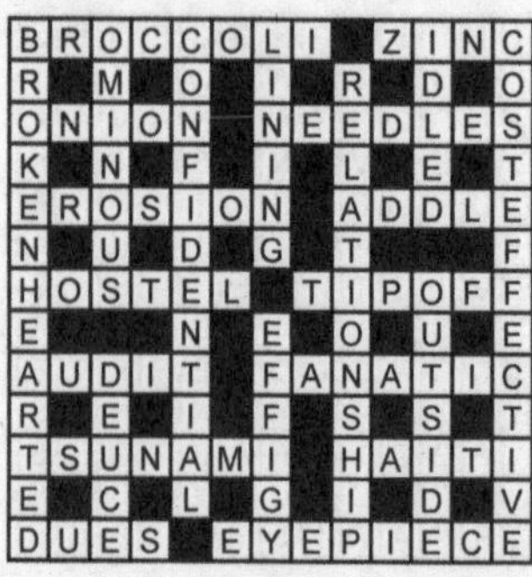

B	R	O	C	C	O	L	I		Z	I	N	C
R		M		O		I		R		D		O
O	N	I	O	N		N	E	E	D	L	E	S
K		N		F		I		L		E		T
E	R	O	S	I	O	N		A	D	D	L	E
N		U		D		G		T				F
H	O	S	T	E	L		T	I	P	O	F	F
E				N		E		O		U		E
A	U	D	I	T		F	A	N	A	T	I	C
R		E		I		F		S		S		T
T	S	U	N	A	M	I		H	A	I	T	I
E		C		L		G		I		D		V
D	U	E	S		E	Y	E	P	I	E	C	E

114

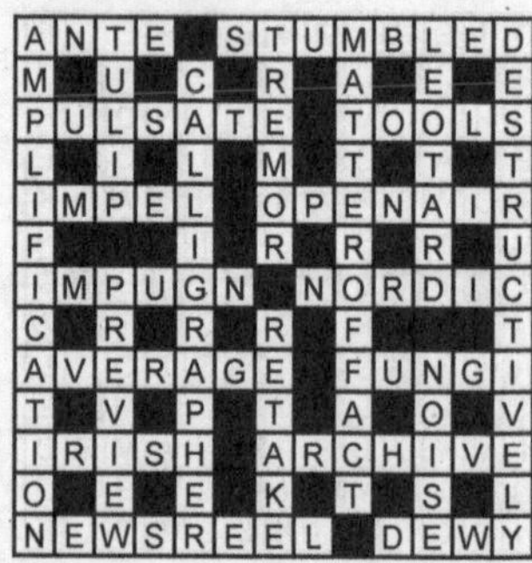

A	N	T	E		S	T	U	M	B	L	E	D
M		U		C		R		A		E		E
P	U	L	S	A	T	E		T	O	O	L	S
L		I		L		M		T		T		T
I	M	P	E	L		O	P	E	N	A	I	R
F				I		R		R		R		U
I	M	P	U	G	N		N	O	R	D	I	C
C		R		R		R		F				T
A	V	E	R	A	G	E		F	U	N	G	I
T		V		P		T		A		O		V
I	R	I	S	H		A	R	C	H	I	V	E
O		E		E		K		T		S		L
N	E	W	S	R	E	E	L		D	E	W	Y

115

I	N	C	H		A	D	D	I	T	I	O	N
N		L		I		I		N		L		O
F	L	O	U	N	C	E		C	O	L	O	N
I		U		S		S		O		I		A
N	O	T		T		E		R	E	C	A	P
I				R	U	L	E	R		I		P
T		S		U				I		T		E
E		I		C	L	I	N	G				A
S	P	L	I	T		N		I		B	A	R
I		I		I		F		B		A		A
M	A	C	H	O		O	I	L	S	K	I	N
A		O		N		R		E		E		C
L	O	N	E	S	O	M	E		B	R	I	E

116

	C	H	O	L	E	S	T	E	R	O	L	
C		E		I		I		L		F		D
O	A	R		V	A	G	U	E		F		I
N		T		E		H		G	U	L	L	S
G	A	Z	E	D		T		I		O		P
R					E	S	C	A	L	A	T	E
E		S		R				C		D		N
S	E	C	R	E	T	L	Y					S
S		A		L		E		C	O	B	R	A
M	O	T	T	O		N		H		I		B
A		T		A	N	G	L	E		N	I	L
N		E		D		T		E		G		E
	G	R	A	S	S	H	O	P	P	E	R	

117

B	O	U	N	C	E	R	S		S	P	U	R
U		K		O		O		A		A		E
S	T	R	U	M		E	X	C	I	T	E	S
H		A		B				K		I		I
	D	I	S	I	N	G	E	N	U	O	U	S
L		N		N		O		O				T
A	Y	E		A	R	R	O	W		B	O	O
C				T		S		L		E		R
R	E	Q	U	I	R	E	M	E	N	T	S	
O		U		O				D		W		P
S	C	A	N	N	E	D		G	R	E	B	E
S		K		S		O		E		E		N
E	V	E	R		S	T	U	D	E	N	T	S

118

U	N	D	O		H	A	N	D	C	U	F	F
N		E		A		D		E		N		O
S	O	A	N	D	S	O		L	O	W	E	R
Y		L		M		R		I		I		G
M	A	T		O		E		G	E	N	R	E
P				N	O	R	T	H		D		T
A		C		I				T		S		F
T		O		S	T	U	F	F				U
H	A	R	S	H		T		U		A	I	L
E		P		M		O		L		M		N
T	H	O	S	E		P	I	L	L	A	G	E
I		R		N		I		Y		Z		S
C	L	A	P	T	R	A	P		F	E	E	S

119

H	I	R	I	N	G		S		B		R	
O		E			A	C	H	I	E	V	E	R
B	O	B			L		U		S		P	
N		U	P	H	E	L	D		M	I	L	L
O		F			S		D		I		A	
B	U	F	F	S		B	E	T	R	A	Y	S
			O		T		R		C			
F	E	A	R	F	U	L		W	H	A	R	F
	U		E		G		B			D		L
S	C	A	N		G	R	O	T	T	O		O
	L		A		I		A			R	A	W
D	I	A	M	O	N	D	S			N		E
	D		E		G		T	E	A	S	E	R

120

S	A	S	H		B	E	C	A	L	M	E	D
O		Y		R		L		P		I		A
C	A	L	D	E	R	A		P	I	L	E	D
I		P		L		T		R		I		S
A	C	H	I	E	V	E	M	E	N	T	S	
B				N		D		H		I		A
L	O	C	A	T	E		D	E	C	A	M	P
E		R		L		N		N				O
	C	A	R	E	L	E	S	S	N	E	S	S
A		C		S		U		I		V		T
L	I	K	E	S		R	I	V	I	E	R	A
G		U		L		O		E		R		T
A	P	P	L	Y	I	N	G		L	Y	R	E

121

	I	M	A	G	I	N	A	T	I	O	N	
C		I		H		E		U		V		B
H	U	M		O	B	E	Y	S		E		E
E		I		U		D		S	T	R	A	W
E	X	C	E	L		E		L		S		I
R					A	D	H	E	R	E	N	T
L		S		B				S		E		C
E	N	T	R	A	N	C	E					H
A		I		N		O		S	W	A	R	M
D	O	M	E	D		G		P		N		E
E		U		A	R	E	N	A		G	I	N
R		L		G		N		I		E		T
	B	I	C	E	N	T	E	N	A	R	Y	

122

	T	H	O	U	G	H	T	L	E	S	S	
T		A		P		O		U		I		A
R		L		S	T	O	R	M		N	U	B
A	L	L	O	W		K		P		C		B
N		W		E		E		S	H	E	A	R
S	T	A	M	P	E	D	E					E
A		Y		T				H		T		V
C					L	I	T	E	R	A	T	I
T	O	W	E	R		N		A		M		A
I		O		A		V		D	R	A	F	T
O	H	M		T	R	O	T	S		R		E
N		A		E		K		E		I		D
	I	N	A	D	V	E	R	T	E	N	T	

123

A	P	S	E		E	F	F	I	C	A	C	Y
S		C		P		A		N		N		O
P	H	A	L	A	N	X		D	I	N	G	Y
E		M		R				I		U		O
R	E	P	E	T	I	T	I	V	E	L	Y	
I				I		H		I		A		O
T	E	E		C	H	I	L	D		R	A	N
Y		M		U		N		U				E
	F	I	E	L	D	G	L	A	S	S	E	S
M		T		A				L		H		I
E	A	T	E	R		B	O	L	L	A	R	D
S		E		L		U		Y		R		E
H	U	R	R	Y	I	N	G		S	P	E	D

124

Q	U	I	T		E	S	C	A	P	E	E	S
U		N		A		E		P		N		E
A	D	D	E	N	D	A		P	E	R	I	L
L		I		N		M		R		O		F
I	D	A	H	O		A	C	E	R	B	I	C
F				U		N		C		E		O
I	N	S	A	N	E		H	I	D	D	E	N
C		T		C		U		A				T
A	G	E	L	E	S	S		T	H	E	T	A
T		T		M		A		I		I		I
I	S	S	U	E		B	R	O	A	D	E	N
O		O		N		L		N		E		E
N	I	N	E	T	I	E	S		T	R	O	D

125

	F	O	R	E	T	H	O	U	G	H	T	
C		U		A		A		R		E		A
A		T		S	L	I	N	G		L	E	T
C	A	D	E	T		L		E		L		M
O		O		E		E		D	U	O	M	O
P	R	O	T	R	U	D	E					S
H		R		N				D		G		P
O					R	E	S	E	A	R	C	H
N	E	W	T	S		N		F		A		E
O		I		E		J		U	P	P	E	R
U	R	N		G	R	O	A	N		H		I
S		D		U		I		C		I		C
	C	Y	B	E	R	N	E	T	I	C	S	

126

R	O	W	S		G	R	A	P	P	L	E	D
E		I		P		U		A		A		I
A	L	S	O	R	A	N		R	I	N	G	S
S		E		O				S		T		H
S	C	R	I	P	T	W	R	I	T	E	R	
E				O		I		M		R		W
S	I	P		R	O	N	D	O		N	O	R
S		O		T		D		N				I
	A	W	E	I	N	S	P	I	R	I	N	G
P		D		O				O		N		G
O	C	E	A	N		J	O	U	R	N	A	L
L		R		A		E		S		E		E
O	B	S	O	L	E	T	E		A	R	I	D

127

	I	M	P	R	E	S	S	I	O	N	S	
W		E		O		L		D		A		S
H	I	D		U	S	U	R	Y		T		K
I		I		G		S		L	A	I	T	Y
T	E	A	S	E		H		L		O		S
E					H	Y	G	I	E	N	I	C
C		D		A				C		S		R
O	V	E	R	P	A	S	S					A
L		F		P		U		T	H	U	M	P
L	E	A	V	E		M		O		N		E
A		C		A	D	M	I	X		F	I	R
R		T		S		I		I		I		S
	D	O	M	E	S	T	I	C	A	T	E	

128

U	P	H	E	A	V	A	L		O	S	L	O
R		A		D		I		I		E		V
G	O	R	E	D		M	A	N	A	T	E	E
E		M		I				T		T		R
	O	F	F	T	H	E	R	E	C	O	R	D
G		U		I		D		R				O
O	W	L		O	D	I	U	M		M	E	N
V				N		C		I		E		E
E	N	C	H	A	N	T	I	N	G	L	Y	
R		I		L				A		L		A
N	O	V	E	L	L	A		B	R	O	N	X
O		I		Y		W		L		W		E
R	I	L	E		R	E	L	E	A	S	E	D

129

R	O	P	E		R	E	A	P	P	E	A	R
O		A		S		L		A		L		E
L	A	N	G	U	I	D		R	E	A	L	M
L		D		B		E		O		T		O
E	X	A	M	S		R	E	C	E	I	P	T
R				T		S		H		O		E
C	A	S	U	A	L		P	I	C	N	I	C
O		N		N		A		A				O
A	Q	U	A	T	I	C		L	E	A	R	N
S		B		I		T		I		C		T
T	I	B	I	A		I	N	S	U	R	E	R
E		E		T		V		M		I		O
R	E	D	D	E	N	E	D		I	D	O	L

130

B	E	F	A	L	L		R		E		C	
A		R			O	V	E	R	T	U	R	E
L	A	Y			G		V		C		E	
T		I	N	T	O	N	E		H	O	A	X
I		N			S		R		I		T	
C	A	G	E	D		S	T	I	N	G	E	R
			U		U		S		G			
B	U	M	P	I	N	G		A	S	K	E	W
	N		H		I		S			E		E
D	E	M	O		T	A	T	T	L	E		D
	A		R		I		U			P	U	G
A	S	S	I	G	N	E	D			E		E
	Y		A		G		S	T	E	R	N	S

131

	A	T	T	E	S	T	A	T	I	O	N	
O		I		D		I		E		B		D
V	E	T		I	N	D	E	X		J		E
E		L		T		I		T	E	E	T	H
R	E	E	K	S		E		I		C		Y
A					I	S	O	L	A	T	E	D
C		D		F				E		S		R
H	A	I	R	L	E	S	S					A
I		L		A		M		T	E	N	E	T
E	L	E	C	T		U		H		E		I
V		M		O	R	D	E	R		W	H	O
E		M		U		G		E		E		N
	E	A	R	T	H	E	N	W	A	R	E	

132

	C	A	T	E	R	P	I	L	L	A	R	
C		F		V		O		O		B		M
L		F		E	V	I	L	S		B	A	A
A	L	I	G	N		S		E		E		K
I		R		I		O		S	T	Y	L	E
R	U	M	I	N	A	N	T					B
V		S		G				G		I		E
O					O	P	T	I	O	N	A	L
Y	A	W	N	S		H		N		S		I
A		I		T		R		S	A	U	C	E
N	I	T		A	B	A	T	E		L		V
T		C		L		S		N		I		E
	C	H	A	L	L	E	N	G	I	N	G	

133

T	O	F	U		S	T	R	A	I	N	E	D
R		R		K		W		M		E		I
I	S	O	L	A	T	E		E	D	G	E	S
A		N		L		A		L		A		T
L	E	D	G	E		K	N	I	T	T	E	R
A				I		S		O		E		E
N	O	B	O	D	Y		A	R	I	S	E	S
D		I		O		P		A				S
E	X	P	O	S	E	S		T	E	M	P	I
R		E		C		Y		I		O		N
R	A	D	I	O		C	O	O	L	I	N	G
O		A		P		H		N		S		L
R	E	L	I	E	V	E	D		S	T	A	Y

134

S	N	I	P	P	E	T	S		O	B	O	E
E		M		E		O		U		A		N
C	A	P	E	R		R	I	N	G	L	E	T
T		I		F				A		S		I
	D	E	C	O	N	G	E	S	T	A	N	T
S		T		R		A		S				L
T	H	Y		M	A	N	N	A		A	T	E
U				A		G		I		W		S
B	U	S	I	N	E	S	S	L	I	K	E	
B		U		C				A		W		S
O	S	P	R	E	Y	S		B	R	A	W	L
R		E		S		E		L		R		U
N	O	R	M		L	A	V	E	N	D	E	R

135

L	O	S	T		R	E	P	U	B	L	I	C
A		A		D		N		N		E		O
C	O	L	L	I	E	R		F	R	O	W	N
K		V		S		A		L		P		F
A	R	E		C		G		A	P	A	C	E
D				O	V	E	R	T		R		C
A		M		U				T		D		T
I		A		R	O	U	S	E				I
S	T	R	U	T		N		R		R	H	O
I		I		E		I		I		E		N
C	A	M	E	O		S	Y	N	A	P	S	E
A		B		U		O		G		E		R
L	I	A	I	S	O	N	S		C	L	A	Y

136

O	G	L	E		D	O	G	F	I	G	H	T
V		U		P		C		L		U		I
E	A	R	S	H	O	T		Y	I	E	L	D
R		K		I		E		I		S		E
A	B	S	O	L	U	T	E	N	E	S	S	
L				H		S		G		E		A
L	E	E	W	A	Y		A	S	I	D	E	S
S		V		R		I		A				C
	C	O	M	M	E	N	S	U	R	A	T	E
A		L		O		J		C		L		N
C	O	V	E	N		E	L	E	C	T	E	D
I		E		I		C		R		E		E
D	E	D	I	C	A	T	E		P	R	O	D

137

M	O	D	E	R	A	T	E		S	C	U	T
U		R		E		R		M		L		A
S	C	A	R	P		A	Z	A	L	E	A	S
I		I		R		V		T		A		T
C	A	N	T	O		E		H		R	Y	E
A		E		D	E	L	V	E				L
L		D		U				M		C		E
C				C	O	N	G	A		O		S
H	O	T		T		I		T	R	U	S	S
A		Y		I		C		I		L		N
I	M	P	R	O	V	E		C	H	O	S	E
R		E		N		L		A		M		S
S	O	D	A		S	Y	L	L	A	B	U	S

138

T	U	B	A		Q	U	A	D	R	A	T	E
Y		L		N		P		I		R		A
P	R	O	F	E	S	S		S	O	C	K	S
E		W		V		E		C		H		E
C	O	N	V	E	N	T	I	O	N	A	L	
A				R		S		R		I		A
S	O	N	A	T	A		E	D	I	C	T	S
T		E		H		I		A				S
	D	E	T	E	R	M	I	N	A	B	L	E
S		D		L		P		T		A		S
H	A	L	V	E		A	T	L	A	S	E	S
I		E		S		L		Y		T		O
P	E	D	E	S	T	A	L		R	E	A	R

139

	S		A		S		T	U	S	S	L	E
S	T	I	L	E	T	T	O			E		V
	R		L		Y		A			E	T	A
M	A	L	I		L	A	S	E	R	S		D
	N		A		I		T			A		E
O	D	D	N	E	S	S		K	I	W	I	S
			C		H		B		N			
R	O	P	E	S		D	I	F	F	U	S	E
I		L			M		G		E		U	
P		A	C	H	I	N	G		R	A	P	T
P	R	Y			N		E		N		P	
L		E			O	B	S	T	A	C	L	E
E	N	D	E	A	R		T		L		E	

140

	P	H	O	T	O	G	R	A	P	H	S	
D		O		O		L		L		O		A
E		T		K	O	A	L	A		W	E	D
V	O	D	K	A		R		R		L		I
A		O		M		E		M	A	S	O	N
L	A	G	G	A	R	D	S					F
U		S		K				D		T		I
A					C	A	M	E	R	O	O	N
T	I	E	R	S		L		S		R		I
I		V		H		I		S	T	O	U	T
O	D	E		A	L	G	A	E		N		U
N		N		K		H		R		T		M
	O	S	T	E	N	T	A	T	I	O	N	

141

M	A	D	E		S	W	A	L	L	O	W	S
I		R		P		A		A		P		I
S	T	A	R	R	E	D		B	I	P	E	D
S		M		E				O		O		E
H	E	A	D	M	I	S	T	R	E	S	S	
A				E		P		A		E		A
P	E	G		D	R	I	F	T		S	I	C
E		R		I		T		O				A
	B	A	T	T	L	E	G	R	O	U	N	D
C		Z		A				I		N		E
H	E	I	S	T		P	R	E	M	I	U	M
E		N		E		U		S		T		I
R	I	G	I	D	I	T	Y		Z	E	T	A

142

	C	A	R	N	I	V	O	R	O	U	S	
A		N		O		A		O		N		R
F	O	G		I	N	G	O	T		C		E
G		E		S		A		T	E	L	L	S
H	I	L	L	Y		R		I		A		U
A					H	Y	P	N	O	S	I	S
N		A		I				G		P		C
I	N	S	O	M	N	I	A					I
S		S		P		N		M	E	R	I	T
T	R	U	C	E		U		I		E		A
A		R		R	E	R	U	N		L	I	T
N		E		I		E		C		I		E
	A	D	O	L	E	S	C	E	N	C	E	

143

	C		S		D		T	U	N	D	R	A
C	O	N	C	R	E	T	E			U		N
	R		R		S		R			S	T	Y
C	O	D	A		C	O	M	B	A	T		W
	N		M		A		S			E		A
J	A	W	B	O	N	E		S	P	R	A	Y
			L		T		R		R			
C	O	P	E	D		R	E	C	E	N	C	Y
U		R			N		F		S		L	
D		A	F	F	A	I	R		A	V	I	D
G	U	Y			V		A		G		N	
E		E			E	M	I	N	E	N	C	E
L	A	R	V	A	L		N		S		H	

144

U	N	A	B	A	T	E	D		T	A	L	C
N		L		V		S		C		I		O
D	E	L	T	A		S	H	O	W	M	A	N
E		O		I		A		U		E		T
R	E	V	E	L	R	Y		N	U	D	G	E
S		E		A		S		T				N
T	H	R	O	B	S		D	E	P	A	R	T
A				I		C		R		P		E
N	E	P	A	L		E	S	C	A	P	E	D
D		E		I		N		L		A		N
I	N	C	I	T	E	S		A	G	R	E	E
N		A		Y		O		I		E		S
G	O	N	G		G	R	U	M	B	L	E	S

145

	P	A	S	S	T	H	E	B	U	C	K	
U		U		L		O		U		O		C
N	O	D		A	U	R	A	L		N		H
O		I		S		N		W	A	D	E	R
B	O	O	T	H		E		A		U		O
S					S	T	A	R	S	I	G	N
E		I		D				K		T		O
R	E	S	P	O	N	S	E					G
V		S		L		E		L	I	V	E	R
A	C	U	T	E		P		U		I		A
N		I		F	U	T	O	N		L	I	P
T		N		U		E		A		L		H
	E	G	A	L	I	T	A	R	I	A	N	

146

F	I	N	S		L	U	K	E	W	A	R	M
O		A		S		N		F		C		A
L	A	C	Q	U	E	R		F	I	R	S	T
L		R		P		I		O		O		E
O	B	E	S	E		P	A	R	T	N	E	R
W				R		E		T		Y		I
T	H	R	O	N	E		A	L	U	M	N	A
H		E		A		T		E				L
R	I	C	H	T	E	R		S	U	S	H	I
O		I		U		A		S		T		S
U	T	T	E	R		C	U	L	P	R	I	T
G		A		A		K		Y		I		I
H	E	L	P	L	E	S	S		E	P	I	C

147

A	T	T	A	C	K	E	D		A	C	E	S
L		U		R		M		B		H		P
L	A	R	G	O		B	A	R	R	I	E	R
Y		M		S		A		E		N		A
	C	O	N	S	E	R	V	A	T	O	R	Y
A		I		E		K		T				I
D	E	L	U	X	E		C	H	O	S	E	N
M				A		T		T		O		G
I	N	C	O	M	P	A	R	A	B	L	Y	
T		O		I		S		K		O		E
T	I	D	I	N	G	S		I	L	I	A	D
E		E		E		E		N		S		G
D	A	S	H		S	L	I	G	H	T	L	Y

148

	A	B	S	T	R	A	C	T	I	O	N	
O		E		A		M		H		U		S
C	O	B		L	O	O	S	E		T		H
C		O		O		E		R	O	D	E	O
U	N	P	I	N		B		A		O		R
R					H	A	P	P	I	E	S	T
R		S		M				Y		S		C
E	N	T	H	A	L	P	Y					H
N		R		N		A		M	A	M	B	A
C	H	I	N	A		R		O		A		N
E		D		G	U	S	T	O		P	I	G
S		E		U		E		N		L		E
	B	R	O	A	D	C	A	S	T	E	R	

149

S	A	G	A	C	I	T	Y		S	E	L	F
A		E		O		H		A		X		I
V	E	N	O	M		R	E	P	T	I	L	E
E		T		M		U		P		S		N
	D	E	M	O	N	S	T	R	A	T	E	D
S		E		N		H		E				I
I	N	L	A	W	S		S	C	A	R	E	S
M				E		P		I		E		H
U	N	C	H	A	R	I	T	A	B	L	E	
L		L		L		G		T		A		T
A	P	O	S	T	L	E		I	M	P	L	Y
T		V		H		O		V		S		P
E	W	E	R		A	N	T	E	C	E	D	E

150

I	R	I	S		C	E	R	B	E	R	U	S
N		S		L		L		I		E		P
C	O	L	L	A	G	E		O	U	T	D	O
O		E		B		C		D		R		N
N	U	T	T	Y		T	R	I	D	E	N	T
S				R		S		V		A		A
I	M	P	A	I	R		B	E	A	T	E	N
D		E		N		O		R				E
E	R	R	A	T	I	C		S	A	L	V	O
R		S		H		E		I		E		U
A	L	I	B	I		L	E	T	T	E	R	S
T		S		N		O		Y		R		L
E	N	T	R	E	A	T	Y		E	S	P	Y

151

	O	B	S	T	R	U	C	T	I	O	N	
S		A		A		N		A		U		D
Y	E	S		B	Y	T	E	S		T		I
N		I		B		I		T	A	L	K	S
D	U	S	T	Y		E		E		I		R
I					E	S	T	R	A	N	G	E
C		F		P				S		E		S
A	L	L	U	R	I	N	G					P
T		U		O		E		B	L	A	M	E
I	N	S	E	T		U		O		C		C
O		T		E	A	R	L	S		H	A	T
N		E		S		A		O		E		S
	B	R	I	T	T	L	E	N	E	S	S	

152

	U		F		Q		T	U	R	B	O	T
A	P	E	R	T	U	R	E			E		H
	K		E		I		N			D	A	Y
R	E	I	N		B	O	D	I	C	E		M
	E		E		B		S			C		U
S	P	A	T	U	L	A		J	O	K	E	S
			I		E		P		F			
P	E	R	C	H		F	U	L	F	I	L	S
U		A			A		N		S		A	
S		G	U	I	D	E	D		H	I	N	D
H	A	G			I		I		O		D	
E		E			O	U	T	C	O	M	E	S
S	E	D	G	E	S		S		T		D	

153

A	R	C	H		O	F	F	I	C	I	A	L
R		R		E		E		N		M		E
T	R	U	F	F	L	E		C	O	P	E	S
I		M		F				O		A		S
S	U	B	S	E	Q	U	E	N	T	L	Y	
T				R		N		S		E		S
R	I	P		V	I	D	E	O		S	O	P
Y		R		E		E		L				L
	C	O	N	S	E	R	V	A	T	I	V	E
S		V		C				B		N		N
T	W	I	C	E		H	O	L	L	A	N	D
A		S		N		E		E		P		I
R	O	O	S	T	I	N	G		S	T	U	D

154

T	E	A	S	P	O	O	N		S	W	A	T
A		C		R		I		U		H		U
P	U	R	G	E		L	I	N	T	E	L	S
S		O		C				D		R		S
	A	B	S	O	L	U	T	E	Z	E	R	O
M		A		N		S		R				C
E	F	T		D	R	I	E	S		I	L	K
R				I		N		T		N		S
C	R	Y	P	T	O	G	R	A	P	H	Y	
I		E		I				F		E		B
F	A	T	U	O	U	S		F	A	R	C	E
U		I		N		H		E		I		T
L	A	S	S		V	E	N	D	E	T	T	A

155

A	N	C	E	S	T	O	R		E	V	E	S
P		A		E		B		N		A		T
P	U	P	I	L		O	V	E	R	L	I	E
R		T		F		I		W		V		A
O	R	I	G	I	N	S		T	R	E	N	D
X		O		N		T		E				F
I	G	N	I	T	E		A	S	T	H	M	A
M				E		C		T		A		S
A	M	B	E	R		A	G	A	I	N	S	T
T		Y		E		E		M		D		N
E	N	L	I	S	T	S		E	N	S	U	E
L		A		T		A		N		O		S
Y	A	W	N		P	R	E	T	E	N	D	S

156

	C	R	I	M	I	N	O	L	O	G	Y	
I		E		O		E		A		A		A
N		T		P	I	L	O	T		P	E	N
S	T	R	O	P		S		E		E		O
T		A		I		O		R	I	S	E	N
R	E	I	G	N	I	N	G					Y
U		N		G				W		O		M
C					H	I	T	H	E	R	T	O
T	A	L	L	Y		C		I		E		U
I		I		U		O		T	O	G	A	S
O	U	T		C	A	N	O	E		A		L
N		H		C		I		S		N		Y
	D	E	M	A	R	C	A	T	I	O	N	

157

P	O	U	N	D	I	N	G		C	L	O	Y
E		N		I		E				O		I
R	A	I	N	S		A	N	I	M	A	T	E
U		S		C		R				T		L
		E		R		L	E	A	S	H	E	D
A	N	X	I	E	T	Y		R		E		I
L				D				B				N
T		S		I		E	R	O	D	I	N	G
E	X	E	R	T	E	D		R		N		
R		R				I		E		T		J
E	L	E	G	A	N	T		T	R	A	D	E
G		N				E		U		C		E
O	M	E	N		O	D	O	M	E	T	E	R

158

I	N	E	X	P	E	R	T		A	R	E	S
N		V		R		O		D		O		T
C	H	I	D	E		A	C	O	L	Y	T	E
R		D		P		R		U		A		R
E	Y	E	S	O	R	E		B	U	L	G	E
D		N		N		D		L				O
U	N	T	I	D	Y		H	E	I	G	H	T
L				E		F		D		A		Y
O	S	C	A	R		O	V	E	R	L	A	P
U		H		A		U		A		I		I
S	C	A	N	N	E	R		L	I	L	A	C
L		I		T		T		E		E		A
Y	A	R	D		C	H	A	R	C	O	A	L

159

E	A	C	H		C	O	N	C	E	R	T	I
X		O		H		V		R		A		M
P	I	C	C	O	L	O		O	X	L	I	P
R		O		P		I		S		L		R
E	V	A	D	E		D	I	S	L	I	K	E
S				L		S		C		E		S
S	W	E	D	E	N		T	O	A	S	T	S
I		X		S		E		U				I
O	P	P	O	S	E	D		N	A	C	H	O
N		L		N		I		T		H		N
I	N	A	N	E		T	E	R	M	I	N	I
S		I		S		O		Y		V		S
M	I	N	I	S	T	R	Y		T	E	A	M

160

D	I	L	E	M	M	A	S		W	E	I	R
I		I		E		I				X		E
A	R	M	E	D		D	E	S	P	O	I	L
L		I		I		I				T		E
		T		C		N	E	E	D	I	N	G
B	A	S	H	I	N	G		N		C		A
L				N				L				T
U		B		E		A	M	I	A	B	L	E
B	L	O	U	S	E	S		G		E		
B		X				S		H		C		E
E	V	I	L	E	Y	E		T	H	A	N	K
R		N				T		E		L		E
Y	O	G	A		T	S	U	N	A	M	I	S

161

	S	U	F	F	I	C	I	E	N	C	Y	
E		N		O		R		M		O		F
S	E	C		C	L	I	M	B		N		O
T		L		U		N		R	E	F	E	R
A	R	E	A	S		G		O		I		G
B					D	E	F	I	A	N	C	E
L		D		C				L		E		T
I	D	E	A	L	I	S	T					M
S		C		U		E		E	X	U	D	E
H	O	O	D	S		S		T		N		N
E		R		T	E	A	C	H		D	U	O
D		U		E		M		I		U		T
	E	M	E	R	G	E	N	C	I	E	S	

162

	S		C		F		H	A	W	K	E	D
C	H	L	O	R	I	N	E			U		E
	O		V		G		A			N	I	B
V	O	T	E		H	O	P	I	N	G		U
	I		N		T		S			F		N
E	N	R	A	G	E	D		C	H	U	C	K
			N		R		H		O			
W	R	O	T	E		H	A	M	L	E	T	S
A		B			S		G		O		A	
S		E	A	R	W	I	G		G	L	I	B
H	A	Y			A		A		R		L	
U		E			N	A	R	R	A	T	E	D
P	E	D	A	L	S		D		M		D	

163

I	N	N	A	T	E	L	Y		T	A	X	I
N		E		O		A		M		L		N
D	O	U	B	T		T	R	E	M	O	L	O
E		T		A		E		A		H		F
S	C	R	O	L	L	S		S	C	A	R	F
C		A		I		T		U				E
R	E	L	A	T	E		O	R	D	A	I	N
I				A		S		E		V		S
B	I	T	E	R		T	I	M	P	A	N	I
A		U		I		R		E		R		V
B	U	F	F	A	L	O		N	A	I	V	E
L		T		N		L		T		C		L
E	L	S	E		B	L	U	S	T	E	R	Y

164

	T		S		F		I	T	S	E	L	F
R	E	S	T	R	A	I	N			M		I
	L		E		I		E			B	U	G
U	L	N	A		N	O	R	M	A	L		H
	E		L		T		T			E		T
B	R	A	I	L	L	E		L	I	M	P	S
			N		Y		F		L			
L	O	D	G	E		B	U	L	L	E	T	S
O		R			G		L		U		I	
O		O	D	I	O	U	S		S	E	N	T
M	A	W			I		O		O		G	
E		S			N	U	M	E	R	A	L	S
D	R	Y	I	N	G		E		Y		E	

165

R	I	D	I	C	U	L	E		B	L	O	C
I		E		A		A		D		E		A
F	E	D	U	P		W	H	O	E	V	E	R
F		U		R		Y		I		E		R
	A	C	C	I	D	E	N	T	A	L	L	Y
O		E		C		R		Y				I
B	O	D	K	I	N		G	O	V	E	R	N
S				O		T		U		M		G
C	I	R	C	U	M	S	C	R	I	B	E	
U		O		S		E		S		R		W
R	I	V	U	L	E	T		E	R	A	S	E
E		E		Y		S		L		C		D
D	I	R	T		S	E	L	F	L	E	S	S

166

R	U	B	Y		P	I	E	C	H	A	R	T
E		O		E		R		O		N		A
S	I	R	O	C	C	O		N	E	X	U	S
I		O		O		N		S		I		K
D	E	N	U	N	C	I	A	T	I	O	N	
U				O		C		R		U		G
A	F	L	A	M	E		C	U	R	S	O	R
L		A		I		B		C				A
	U	N	A	C	C	U	S	T	O	M	E	D
S		K		A		T		I		O		I
K	R	I	L	L		T	R	O	U	N	C	E
E		E		L		O		N		T		N
W	O	R	R	Y	I	N	G		S	H	U	T

167

R	A	S	H		T	E	R	R	I	F	I	C
E		I		M		R		E		O		R
C	E	N	T	A	U	R		M	I	C	R	O
E		E		N		A		U		U		S
P	E	W		U		T		N	E	S	T	S
T				F	L	A	R	E		E		C
I		B		A				R		D		U
V		R		C	U	R	I	A				L
E	X	A	C	T		U		T		P	A	T
N		M		U		S		I		A		U
E	M	B	E	R		T	R	O	U	S	E	R
S		L		E		L		N		T		A
S	H	E	R	R	I	E	S		K	E	E	L

168

	G		S		N		J	E	T	S	A	M
P	R	E	C	L	U	D	E			E		A
	I		H		M		A			V	E	X
G	E	N	E		B	A	N	G	L	E		I
	V		M		E		S			R		M
D	E	V	I	L	R	Y		O	P	E	N	S
			N		S		V		A			
C	O	U	G	H		M	I	R	R	O	R	S
R		N			C		B		T		O	
A		F	E	E	L	E	R		T	U	T	U
T	O	O			A		A		I		A	
E		L			I	N	T	I	M	A	T	E
R	A	D	I	U	M		E		E		E	

169

C	A	F	F	E	I	N	E		A	C	N	E
U		R		N		A		A		R		S
B	L	O	A	T		B	A	S	K	E	T	S
A		T		E				T		E		A
	C	H	O	R	E	O	G	R	A	P	H	Y
C		E		T		G		O				I
L	A	D		A	P	R	O	N		B	U	S
E				I		E		O		I		T
A	S	T	O	N	I	S	H	M	E	N	T	
N		O		I				I		D		H
S	C	R	U	N	C	H		C	A	I	R	O
E		U		G		O		A		N		M
R	E	S	T		E	P	I	L	O	G	U	E

170

D	A	F	T		B	L	A	C	K	O	U	T
A		L		A		A		O		S		U
T	R	A	I	L	E	D		N	O	S	E	S
A		I		L		I		T		I		K
B	E	L	L	I	G	E	R	E	N	C	E	
A				M		S		M		L		T
S	C	R	I	P	T		A	P	I	E	C	E
E		E		O		E		T				N
	O	V	E	R	I	N	D	U	L	G	E	D
E		E		T		A		O		R		E
M	A	N	T	A		B	O	U	D	O	I	R
I		U		N		L		S		U		E
T	R	E	S	T	L	E	S		S	P	U	D

171

	C		S		P		P	U	F	F	E	D
D	A	I	Q	U	I	R	I			I		O
	R		U		T		X			A	P	T
A	R	E	A		C	H	I	E	F	S		T
	O		B		H		E			C		E
S	T	A	B	L	E	S		A	V	O	I	D
			L		R		N		I			
C	O	W	E	D		C	O	N	C	E	D	E
O		A			C		N		I		E	
R		R	U	S	H	E	S		N	E	R	O
G	E	M			U		T		I		I	
I		E			N	O	O	N	T	I	D	E
S	T	R	U	C	K		P		Y		E	

172

E	V	I	L		E	S	O	T	E	R	I	C
X		N		E		V		R		O		A
P	A	C	K	A	G	E		A	D	A	P	T
A		U		V		L		N		M		E
N	E	R	V	E		T	O	S	S	I	N	G
S				S		E		M		N		O
I	N	S	I	D	E		F	I	N	G	E	R
V		E		R		L		S				I
E	N	C	L	O	S	E		S	O	N	I	C
N		L		P		S		I		I		A
E	Q	U	I	P		S	T	O	I	C	A	L
S		D		E		O		N		H		L
S	T	E	E	R	I	N	G		D	E	N	Y

173

H	E	A	D	G	E	A	R		P	A	I	L
E		R		O		L		O		B		I
A	P	R	I	L		L	E	V	Y	I	N	G
T		A		D		E		E		D		H
	U	N	D	E	R	G	A	R	M	E	N	T
C		G		N		E		E				E
R	E	E	K	E	D		S	M	E	A	R	S
E				A		M		P		C		T
D	E	M	O	G	R	A	P	H	I	C	S	
I		O		L		K		A		R		E
B	E	L	I	E	V	E		S	T	U	N	G
L		A		S		D		I		E		G
E	R	R	S		C	O	N	S	I	S	T	S

174

M	E	R	M	A	I	D	S		F	I	L	M
A		E		E		E		O		G		I
N	E	V	E	R		N	I	B	B	L	E	S
U		I		O		I		S		O		C
F	R	E	E	D	O	M		E	P	O	C	H
A		W		Y		S		R				I
C	A	S	I	N	G		A	V	I	A	T	E
T				A		R		A		M		V
U	N	A	R	M		A	R	T	D	E	C	O
R		L		I		N		I		R		U
I	N	D	U	C	T	S		O	M	I	T	S
N		E		S		O		N		C		L
G	I	R	L		E	M	I	S	S	A	R	Y

175

D	O	L	T		A	R	G	U	A	B	L	Y
R		A		P		E		N		I		E
A	M	B	I	E	N	T		A	D	O	P	T
W		E		R		U		T		L		I
I	L	L	U	S	T	R	A	T	I	O	N	
N				E		N		R		G		E
G	E	N	E	V	A		L	A	R	Y	N	X
S		A		E		O		C				C
	U	N	P	R	O	F	I	T	A	B	L	E
U		N		A		F		I		O		S
R	E	I	G	N		E	N	V	I	O	U	S
D		E		C		N		E		K		E
U	N	S	T	E	A	D	Y		A	S	P	S

176

C	A	S	K		B	A	R	N	A	C	L	E
O		T		N		D		U		R		A
N	I	R	V	A	N	A		R	E	E	F	S
S		A		R		P		S		W		Y
T	O	P	I	C		T	H	E	R	M	A	L
E				I		S		R		A		I
R	A	D	I	S	H		H	Y	E	N	A	S
N		E		S		B		R				T
A	T	E	L	I	E	R		H	I	N	G	E
T		P		S		A		Y		I		N
I	N	E	P	T		Z	A	M	B	E	Z	I
O		S		I		E		E		C		N
N	O	T	I	C	I	N	G		B	E	R	G

177

	B	I	B	L	I	O	P	H	I	L	E	
A		N		O		C		O		E		B
L		H		U	S	U	R	P		M	O	O
T	R	U	S	T		L		E		U		M
E		M		I		A		S	C	R	U	B
R	E	A	S	S	U	R	E					A
N		N		H				H		E		R
A					U	N	H	A	R	M	E	D
T	A	M	E	S		U		N		B		M
I		A		Y		G		D	R	A	P	E
V	A	N		R	A	G	E	S		R		N
E		G		U		E		E		G		T
	C	O	M	P	U	T	A	T	I	O	N	

178

A	N	G	R	I	E	S	T		S	C	A	R
D		R		N		L		D		R		E
A	B	O	U	T		U	S	E	L	E	S	S
M		W		E		M		V		P		E
	E	N	T	R	E	P	R	E	N	E	U	R
O		U		C		S		L				V
P	E	P	P	E	R		T	O	P	P	L	E
A				P		P		P		A		D
Q	U	E	S	T	I	O	N	M	A	R	K	
U		L		I		E		E		T		C
E	N	D	M	O	S	T		N	E	I	G	H
L		E		N		R		T		N		A
Y	A	R	N		E	Y	E	S	I	G	H	T

179

	P	E	C	U	L	I	A	R	I	T	Y	
A		D		N		D		I		O		C
U		I		W	H	I	R	L		P	E	A
D	I	T	T	O		O		E		A		N
A		I		U		M		D	A	Z	E	D
C	O	O	L	N	E	S	S					L
I		N		D				E		A		E
O					D	R	E	A	D	F	U	L
U	N	C	U	T		U		R		R		I
S		O		I		S		D	O	I	N	G
L	A	W		M	O	T	O	R		C		H
Y		E		I		I		U		A		T
	P	R	E	D	I	C	A	M	E	N	T	

180

S	T	E	A	D	I	L	Y		C	A	M	P
I		L		I		O		P		L		L
T	R	I	A	L		T	R	O	U	B	L	E
S		S		A				S		U		A
	H	I	P	P	O	P	O	T	A	M	U	S
M		O		I		O		G				I
I	N	N		D	R	I	E	R		F	I	N
S				A		S		A		E		G
H	E	A	R	T	R	E	N	D	I	N	G	
M		M		I				U		C		C
A	M	P	H	O	R	A		A	R	I	E	L
S		L		N		W		T		N		A
H	E	E	D		A	L	L	E	R	G	E	N

181

	T	R	I	B	U	L	A	T	I	O	N	
R		E		U		E		I		R		A
U		M		R	O	T	O	R		C	U	P
L	E	A	K	Y		T		E		A		P
E		N		I		E		D	I	S	C	O
O	R	D	I	N	A	R	Y					I
F		S		G				K		F		N
T					R	A	I	N	C	O	A	T
H	O	L	E	S		L		I		R		M
U		A		L		U		T	I	L	D	E
M	A	R		A	D	M	I	T		O		N
B		V		N		N		E		R		T
	F	A	C	T	F	I	N	D	I	N	G	

182

F	O	X	Y		T	R	A	I	N	E	R	S
E		Y		E		O		N		X		O
R	E	L	A	X	E	D		A	S	P	E	N
O		E		P				D		E		S
C	O	M	M	E	N	C	E	M	E	N	T	
I				R		E		I		S		M
T	A	P		I	D	L	E	S		E	G	O
Y		R		M		L		S				R
	P	O	L	E	P	O	S	I	T	I	O	N
O		F		N				B		D		I
W	H	I	S	T		B	I	L	L	I	O	N
E		T		A		A		E		O		G
D	I	S	P	L	A	Y	S		I	M	P	S

183

U	S	E	S		T	R	A	I	T	O	R	S
N		R		M		H		N		C		U
D	I	E	T	A	R	Y		T	R	U	M	P
E		C		S		M		E		L		E
R	A	T	E	S		E	A	R	L	I	E	R
E				P		D		P		S		F
S	A	H	A	R	A		B	R	U	T	A	L
T		E		O		A		E				U
I	M	P	E	D	E	D		T	E	M	P	O
M		A		U		J		I		O		U
A	T	T	I	C		O	B	V	I	O	U	S
T		I		E		I		E		S		L
E	N	C	O	D	I	N	G		D	E	F	Y

184

I	N	T	R	E	P	I	D		E	T	C	H
N		O		L		N		S		I		Y
E	L	I	D	E		H	I	L	L	T	O	P
X		L		C		E		E		A		E
P	O	I	N	T	E	R		D	I	N	E	R
E		N		R		E		G				C
R	E	G	I	O	N		F	E	N	C	E	R
I				L		O		H		H		I
E	D	I	F	Y		P	E	A	S	A	N	T
N		D		S		P		M		N		I
C	H	O	R	I	Z	O		M	A	G	I	C
E		L		S		S		E		E		A
D	U	S	K		R	E	P	R	I	S	A	L

185

R	U	L	E		E	D	U	C	A	T	O	R
A		A		G		R		O		O		O
M	I	S	E	R	L	Y		N	O	R	M	S
P		E		A				S		N		Y
A	G	R	I	C	U	L	T	U	R	A	L	
R				I		A		L		D		H
T	W	O		O	U	G	H	T		O	W	E
S		P		U		E		A				E
	O	U	T	S	T	R	E	T	C	H	E	D
O		L		N				I		A		L
R	E	E	V	E		P	R	O	F	I	L	E
C		N		S		H		N		K		S
A	R	T	I	S	T	I	C		J	U	G	S

186

S	O	R	T		F	O	X	H	O	L	E	S
O		E		H		R		Y		O		U
P	I	A	N	O	L	A		P	O	W	E	R
H		D		M		T		O		L		R
I	C	Y		E		O		T	R	I	P	E
S				L	A	R	C	H		F		P
T		A		E				E		E		T
I		I		S	H	O	U	T				I
C	A	R	P	S		F		I		P	O	T
A		D		N		F		C		A		I
T	H	R	E	E		S	H	A	M	P	O	O
E		O		S		E		L		A		U
D	E	P	O	S	I	T	S		A	L	P	S

187

	N	A	T	I	O	N	A	L	I	S	T	
I		Z		N		O		A		E		A
N		I		H	A	V	E	N		W	I	G
C	O	M	M	A		I		K		E		G
O		U		B		C		Y	O	D	E	L
R	E	T	A	I	N	E	R					O
R		H		T				D		B		M
E					T	R	E	A	S	U	R	E
C	A	R	D	S		O		R		R		R
T		O		T		C		K	A	R	M	A
L	U	G		E	R	O	D	E		I		T
Y		U		E		C		S		T		E
	R	E	A	P	P	O	R	T	I	O	N	

188

P	O	P	E		G	R	A	D	U	A	T	E
E		O		D		E		E		R		V
R	A	S	H	E	R	S		M	E	R	G	E
P		I		S		T		O		I		R
E	A	T		C		E		N	O	V	E	L
N				R	I	D	E	S		E		A
D		A		I				T		D		S
I		L		P	A	L	E	R				T
C	U	B	I	T		E		A		C	H	I
U		A		I		A		B		R		N
L	I	N	G	O		S	E	L	L	I	N	G
A		I		N		E		E		M		L
R	H	A	P	S	O	D	Y		V	E	R	Y

189

U	P	H	O	L	D	E	R		A	R	I	A
N		O		O		M		C		I		U
R	I	T	E	S		B	L	O	W	O	U	T
E		H		T		E		N		J		O
C	R	E	E	P	E	R		Q	U	A	L	M
O		A		R		S		U				A
V	I	D	E	O	S		W	I	D	G	E	T
E				P		S		S		O		I
R	U	P	E	E		T	I	T	A	N	I	C
A		L		R		A		A		D		A
B	L	U	S	T	E	R		D	R	O	L	L
L		M		Y		C		O		L		L
E	P	E	E		P	H	A	R	M	A	C	Y

190

B	Y	P	L	A	Y		S		C		A	
A		A			E	X	P	L	A	I	N	S
C	O	N			L		U		L		K	
K		A	M	U	L	E	T		A	X	L	E
U		M			S		T		M		E	
P	L	A	C	E		R	E	G	A	T	T	A
			A		C		R		R			
I	S	S	U	E	R	S		P	I	T	C	H
	P		S		O		H			R		E
F	R	E	E		Q	U	A	R	T	O		R
	E		W		U		T			J	A	M
J	A	P	A	N	E	S	E			A		I
	D		Y		T		S	O	N	N	E	T

191

	I		R		A		H	I	C	C	U	P
A	N	G	E	L	I	C	A			H		R
	N		V		M		I			A	C	E
C	A	V	A		L	O	L	L	O	P		F
	T		M		E		S			E		I
D	E	S	P	I	S	E		H	E	L	I	X
			E		S		P		A			
H	E	A	D	Y		F	A	I	R	W	A	Y
U		B			W		D		T		P	
M		R	E	A	R	E	D		H	A	L	E
A	G	O			O		O		I		O	
N		A			N	I	C	K	N	A	M	E
E	N	D	I	N	G		K		G		B	

192

P	L	O	P		T	E	R	R	A	P	I	N
R		C		U		K		E		R		O
E	N	T	E	N	T	E		P	L	O	T	S
D		E		F				O		L		E
I	N	T	R	O	V	E	R	S	I	O	N	
C				R		M		S		N		P
T	I	C		G	L	A	Z	E		G	E	L
S		L		I		I		S				A
	C	O	N	V	A	L	E	S	C	E	N	T
E		S		A				I		X		O
B	L	U	R	B		S	C	O	R	P	I	O
B		R		L		P		N		E		N
S	K	E	L	E	T	A	L		I	L	L	S

193

H	A	N	D	L	I	N	G		T	U	N	A
I		U		A		E				P		N
V	A	N	E	S		U	T	T	E	R	L	Y
E		C		S		T				E		W
		I		I		E	P	I	T	A	P	H
B	O	O	S	T	E	R		M		R		E
L				U				B				R
A		A		D		N	A	R	R	A	T	E
C	H	I	M	E	R	A		O		L		
K		R				S		G		P		R
E	M	B	A	R	K	S		L	E	A	C	H
N		A				A		I		C		E
S	A	G	O		A	U	T	O	M	A	T	A

194

B	A	S	E	B	A	L	L		O	P	A	L
O		A		O		E		S		R		I
U	N	D	I	D		D	R	A	W	I	N	G
N		D		Y		G		C		S		H
T	R	E	M	B	L	E		R	E	M	I	T
I		N		U		R		I				F
F	O	S	S	I	L		A	L	K	A	L	I
U				L		A		E		L		N
L	I	P	I	D		L	A	G	G	I	N	G
N		U		I		B		I		G		E
E	X	P	A	N	S	E		O	W	N	E	R
S		A		G		D		U		E		E
S	E	E	N		L	O	P	S	I	D	E	D

195

	B		B		E		G	A	U	G	E	D
M	A	R	A	U	D	E	R			A		U
	Z		C		U		U			B	O	G
H	A	W	K		C	O	B	W	E	B		O
	A		F		A		S			L		U
P	R	E	L	A	T	E		G	U	E	S	T
			I		E		M		B			
W	A	S	P	S		M	A	T	I	N	E	E
H		L			S		S		Q		L	
E		O	U	N	C	E	S		U	N	I	T
R	O	W			U		I		I		C	
R		E			D	O	V	E	T	A	I	L
Y	O	D	E	L	S		E		Y		T	

196

H	U	S	K		O	B	S	T	R	U	C	T
I		C		D		O		H		G		E
G	E	O	L	O	G	Y		O	G	L	E	S
H		W		M				R		I		T
S	E	L	F	E	M	P	L	O	Y	E	D	
E				S		R		U		S		E
A	S	H		T	Y	I	N	G		T	I	P
S		A		I		O		H				I
	E	L	E	C	T	R	I	F	Y	I	N	G
V		C		A				A		T		R
I	D	Y	L	L		S	Y	R	I	A	N	A
S		O		L		O		E		L		P
A	N	N	O	Y	I	N	G		M	Y	T	H

197

C	Y	B	O	R	G		C		I		E	
A		U			O	N	E	O	N	O	N	E
R	I	G			O		L		S		M	
T		L	A	W	F	U	L		T	R	E	E
E		E			Y		A		R		S	
L	I	S	T	S		G	R	O	U	C	H	Y
			E		B		S		C			
A	S	H	T	R	A	Y		S	T	O	O	D
	Q		H		R		A			P		A
M	U	T	E		R	E	G	I	M	E		C
	I		R		A		L			R	O	T
A	R	P	E	G	G	I	O			A		Y
	T		D		E		W	E	A	S	E	L

198

C	A	G	E		K	E	Y	B	O	A	R	D
H		R		C		V		E		S		A
A	L	A	N	I	N	E		S	O	P	P	Y
R		N		R				P		E		S
I	N	T	E	R	F	E	R	E	N	C	E	
S				O		J		C		T		B
M	A	G		C	R	E	S	T		S	K	I
A		E		U		C		A				C
	D	O	G	M	A	T	I	C	A	L	L	Y
B		R		U				L		O		C
L	E	G	A	L		G	L	E	E	F	U	L
U		I		U		O		D		T		E
R	O	A	D	S	I	D	E		E	Y	E	S

199

M	O	B	S		C	A	N	B	E	R	R	A
I		U		U		R		U		O		L
S	T	R	A	N	G	E		R	A	M	P	S
S		M		I		N		G		A		O
P	L	A	I	N	S	A	I	L	I	N	G	
E				T		S		A		I		W
N	A	I	L	E	D		B	R	O	A	C	H
D		N		R		E		A				I
	C	H	E	E	R	F	U	L	N	E	S	S
A		A		S		F		A		N		T
D	E	L	F	T		U	N	R	A	V	E	L
D		E		E		S		M		O		E
S	H	R	E	D	D	E	D		E	Y	E	D

200

A	D	V	E	R	B		P		A		K	
T		E			A	C	R	I	M	O	N	Y
T	U	X			T		E		B		O	
A		I	N	C	O	M	E		R	A	T	E
C		N			N		N		O		T	
H	I	G	H	S		J	E	R	S	E	Y	S
			Y		A		D		I			
S	A	R	D	I	N	E		C	A	D	R	E
	G		R		N		M			E		X
S	H	O	O		E	V	O	L	V	E		T
	A		G		L		N			P	E	R
A	S	T	E	R	I	S	K			E		A
	T		N		D		S	P	I	R	E	S